# TOMBOY SURVIVAL GUIDE

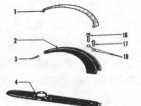
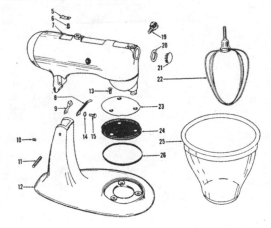

# TOMBOY SURVIVAL GUIDE

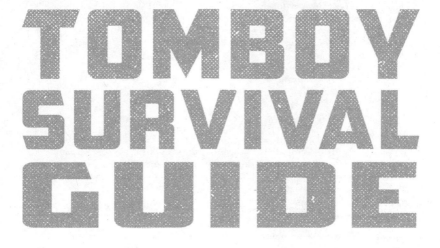

-/---/--/···/---/--·--/
···/··-—/·-—·/····—/··/···-—/·-—/·-—··/
—-—·/·-—/··/—··/·/

## IVAN COYOTE

··/···-—/·-/-·/
—-·-—·/·---/---··-·/---/-—/·/

ARSENAL
PULP PRESS
·VANCOUVER

TOMBOY SURVIVAL GUIDE
Copyright © 2016 by Ivan Coyote

THIRD PRINTING: 2018

ARSENAL PULP PRESS
Suite 202 – 211 East Georgia St.
Vancouver, BC V6A 1Z6
Canada
*arsenalpulp.com*

The publisher gratefully acknowledges the support of the Canada Council for the Arts and the British Columbia Arts Council for its publishing program, and the Government of Canada (through the Canada Book Fund) and the Government of British Columbia (through the Book Publishing Tax Credit Program) for its publishing activities.

"What We Pray For (The Tomboy Hymn)": based on the hymn by Arthur Seymour Sullivan; Lyrics by Veda Hille, taken from discussions with Alison Gorman, Sally Zori, Pebbles Willekes, and Ivan Coyote

"Will You Come With Me?": Music by Veda Hille, lyrics by Veda Hille, taken from discussions with Alison Gorman, Sally Zori, Pebbles Willekes, and Ivan Coyote

Efforts have been made to locate copyright holders of source material wherever possible. The publisher welcomes hearing from any copyright holders of material used in this book who have not been contacted.

Cover and text design by Oliver McPartlin
Cover illustration by Dan Bushnell
Edited by Brian Lam

Printed and bound in Canada

Library and Archives Canada Cataloguing in Publication:
Coyote, Ivan E. (Ivan Elizabeth), 1969-, author
    Tomboy survival guide / Ivan E. Coyote.

Issued in print and electronic formats.
ISBN 978-1-55152-656-0 (paperback).—ISBN 978-1-55152-657-7 (html)

    1. Coyote, Ivan E. (Ivan Elizabeth), 1969-. 2. Transgender people—Identity. 3. Tomboys—Canada—Biography. I. Title.

HQ77.8.C69A3 2016          306.76'8092          C2016-904381-9
                                                C2016-904382-7

I dedicate this book to Alison Gorman, Pebbles Willekes, and Sally Zori, the other three members of our all-tomboy band, for their talent and heart. Many of the stories in this book have been put to their music and brought to the stage. This has given these words another life and other dimensions, and for that I will always be grateful.

I would also like to dedicate this book to Leanne Powers, Soo Jeong, Roxanne Duncan, and Lee Del Vecchio. Behind, beside, in front of, and surrounding these brave tomboys there is a friend, a wife, a non-wife, and a husbutch. I would like to thank them all for their love, support, bathroom accompaniment, and for seeing us and being our family. Without you there would be a big empty space shaped just like you.

Lastly and especially, I dedicate this book to Patricia Daws, my mother, my friend, my mentor, and my first hero. The words love and respect are not big enough to hold everything that I feel for you. You were with me, in my blood and in my heart, while I wrote every word.

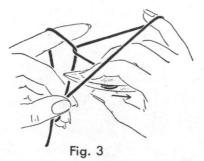

**Fig. 3**

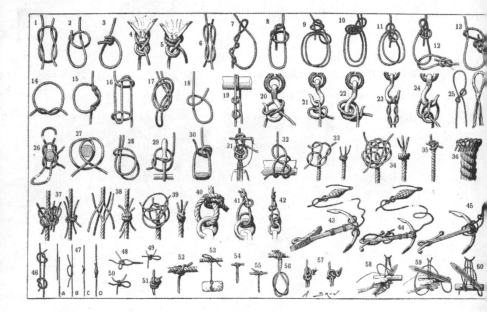

# CONTENTS

Fig. 3.

"I was not ladylike, nor was I manly. I was something else altogether. There were so many different ways to be beautiful."
—Michael Cunningham, *A Home at the End of the World*

I'm waiting in the insurance place to renew my plates, along with a woman and her daughter, about five years old. The kid keeps talking to me, asking me stuff, showing me her Lego helicopter. "Leave her be," the mom says. The kid looks right at me. "I don't think he is a lady," she says. "I think he is a man with very pretty eyes."

# NOT MY SON

I'm trying to think back to the very first time I knew. I probably knew before I even knew what knowing was, but the first time I really *remember*, I was maybe five years old. It was summer in the Yukon, I remember that, there is no mistaking summer in the Yukon. It was early in the evening when the shadows fall long and sideways under the midnight sun, stretching slender from the tips of my sneakers all the way across the dusty parking lot next to the Qwanlin Mall downtown. I was wearing a baseball hat that was too big for me, I had to heat up a safety pin and melt another hole in the plastic strap at the back to make it small enough to stay on my head at all. My mom and I had just finished grocery shopping and our cart was loaded down with brown paper bags. I held the glass door open for her to push the cart through.

A tourist man wearing tourist shorts and a tourist shirt was on his way in to the Super Valu, and he stopped to let us exit past him. "You're a good boy, son, to help your mama like that," he drawled at me.

My chest puffed up like a little rooster and I stood taller, like I thought maybe a soldier would, or a doorman, someone with a uniform and a purpose. Nodded quick, without smiling.

My mom sighed and squinted into the sun in his direction. "She's not my son, she is my daughter," she told him, without any edge in her voice, just the facts.

"Pardon me, ma'am, my apologies." He cocked an eyebrow like a question mark at me, and then headed inside.

My mom didn't mention the incident again, ever, but I remembered it. Rolled it around in my head after like a small, smooth pebble. I liked being mistaken for a boy. Liked how it meant I was expected to do things: to stand up tall, open doors, be strong, to help my mother. How I got approving nods from tall men with accents from other countries. I didn't know why it made my heart sing loud to itself that a stranger thought I was a boy. It just did. Made me feel like he could look inside me and see some part of the truth of me in there.

But it did make me inexplicably sad that a stranger could see me, and my own family could not.

The summer I turned six was the first time I intentionally passed as a boy. It had always just happened incidentally, accidentally, before then, before that July and those summer swimming lessons at the Lions pool. My mom had made the mistake of buying me a bikini. The bottoms fit like circa 1974 polyester shorts, blue with red pockets, and the top part was a little tank top, red with blue pockets. It was pretty butch, come to think of it, as bikinis go. It was so easy, that first day. I didn't give it too much thought, really, I just didn't wear the top part. Left it scrunched into a ball and shoved deep into the toe of my running shoe at the bottom of a rent-it-for-a-quarter locker. I pinned the key with the hard plastic orange number on it to the waistband of my trunks and padded barefoot out to the side of the pool. I fell into line with the boys that first day, and it only got easier after that. The short form of the birth name my parents had given me was androgynous enough to allow my charade to continue through all six weeks of swimming lessons. I didn't get busted until report card day. "'He has progressed through all of the requirements of his beginners class and is ready to proceed on to his level two'?" My mom read aloud in the car in the parking lot outside of the pool, shaking her head slowly. "I knew that bikini was a mistake from the get-go."

I stared at the toes of my sneakers and said nothing. I didn't understand why it was easier to do cannonballs and tread water without a flotation device without being afraid of the deep end when nobody expected you to be afraid. It just was. I still remember that too-good-to-be-real feeling of the water sliding over my bare chest. It's not like I thought I was a real boy. I just knew I was not really a girl.

I was never taught to believe that women were inferior, just different. In fact, I was raised in a family of mostly single mothers. My maternal grandfather was a drunk who died when I was nine, shriveled and yellow and full of bitter. My gran had three jobs and kept everybody fed and spotless and patched and darned and in school, and showed us all with her bent back and arthritic fingers curled into her palms what hard work was. My other grandfather had excised himself from his family and responsibilities in exchange for the sun and winterless shores of New Zealand, and it was well-known family lore that he couldn't hold down a decent job or treat a woman right.

The women in my family handled most of the practical details of everyday life. Men were skilled at some things, at the same time as being inexplicably incapable of performing other seemingly simple tasks. I grew up believing that men were faulty creatures, a little untrustworthy, childlike, even. They needed a woman around to keep them on the tracks. To swipe their paycheque out of their calloused hands right after work every other Thursday before they went and spent it on something stupid like a snowmobile, or a bigger boat. Men swore at the table and were prone to fighting on account of dubious slights, and hardly any of them even knew how to work the washing machine. If you needed something done right, or to get picked up on time by someone after gymnastics or whatever, it was always best if that someone was a woman. Men were mostly just good for fixing or building things and for hauling firewood. A lot of this work happened out of town in the bush somewhere, or in camps my dad and uncles talked about on their four days off. This work seemed far away, and out of mind, and had little to do with the day in front of us. It was just the way it was.

I didn't not want to be a girl because I had been told that they were weaker or somehow lesser than boys. It was never that simple. I didn't even really actively not want to be like the other girls. I just knew. I just always knew that I wasn't. I couldn't. I would never be.

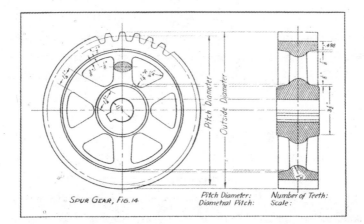

SPUR GEAR, FIG. 14                     Pitch Diameter:          Number of Teeth:
                                       Diametral Pitch:         Scale :

My grandmother Flo was not a cuddly woman. She was far more likely to cuff the back of your head than she was to pat the top of it. Maybe that is why this memory jumps out so stark and solo in my head.

My gran had a wicker chair with a removable cushion on it, and for years that chair belonged to her dog Pug. Pug was a pug, of course, and I guess that was a good enough name for a dog. Pug slept most of the day away in that chair and if you tried to sit next to her or even accidentally got too close to her chair while on your way to the kitchen or the back door, she would snap and bite at the air in front of your face, sometimes catching your bottom lip or a piece of your cheek, and my gran would swoop out of the kitchen with the broom in her hand and accuse you of teasing that poor old hound, screeching at you to just leave the dog in peace. Before my grandfather died he would fry up a bit of fresh liver and chop it into tiny bits, and then blow on it until it was cool enough for Pug to snarfle and gulp down. My uncles would roll their eyes and complain that goddammit the old man never bothered to cook anything for anyone else. Then my grandfather got sick and withered and died, and then Pug died, too. I was too young for funerals when my grandpa died, but I remember my aunts sobbing and leaning on each other when that grouchy old stinky dog got buried in the back yard under the wild rose bush, between the slumping shed and the poplar tree.

After Pug was gone, my gran unzipped the cover off of the cushion from the old wicker chair and washed it and hung it on the line, and hung the pillow over the railing on the back porch and pounded the dust out of it with an old ping pong paddle. One afternoon when all the other kids were out playing but I got to stay in because I had a bad cold, she sat back in that chair and had herself a proper smoke, and then patted her lap for me to come and sit in it. This was rare enough that I remember every detail: her cardigan pulled closed and buttoned around her spindly frame, her cigarette still smoldering a little in the green glass ashtray on the side table, the spoon rack in the shape of the Yukon that my uncle made for her when he was in rehab hanging on the wall over her shoulder.

I climbed up into her bony lap and tried to balance there without letting my full weight rest on her thighs. She wrapped one of her gnarly-old-smoker-lady-bingo-fingered hands around my hip, and opened her other hand in front of me, palm up. Shining in the wrinkled bowl of her palm was a silver medallion.

"This is for St. Jude," she told me, leaving a little space in between each of her words so I knew this was serious. "He is the patron saint of hopeless causes. I want you to have this. We will pin it inside your new jeans jacket, right over your heart. He will be your patron saint. You can pray to him whenever you need to. Some of us have hard roads, but the Lord never gives anyone a burden without also giving them a gift. Your job is to find out what that gift is and use it, y'hear me? God doesn't make mistakes. Never forget that. You are exactly who God meant you to be. You listen to your old gran, there's a good girl. Do you want a hot dog for lunch? Now how does that sound?"

I still have that St. Jude medallion. I kept it for years on a key ring with a couple of others I collected over the years: a solid silver St. Christopher's for travellers that I found in a thrift store in North Vancouver, and a St. Catherine's, the patron saint for unmarried women. They were in the right front pocket of my jeans the day my house burned down in 2005, so, unlike most of my belongings I started out that day with, I still have them, even more precious to me now because they escaped with me. I have a little wooden box on my dresser in the bedroom. I keep them in there.

In 1981 my grandmother announced that she was tired of the long Yukon winters, and put her little house on Alexander Street up for sale. It was tucked in right next to the clay cliffs in downtown Whitehorse. She got a decent price for it and bought herself a small house in Nanaimo, on Vancouver Island. It was halfway down a little dead-end road named Rosamond Street, in a working-class neighbourhood of the blue-collar pulp mill town. She brought me and my little sister Carrie and my younger cousins Christopher and Dan with her for that first summer, because my mom was going back to school and my aunt was going through a divorce, and both women needed all of us out of their hair for a while. We were eleven, nine, eight, and seven years old.

Carrie was sixteen months younger than me, and we shared very little other than the wall that separated our bedrooms. I kept my room spotless, my books in order from tallest to smallest, my toys stowed in the wooden trunk my dad had built me. My mom had to inspect my sister's room at least once a week to make sure she didn't have half a moldy sandwich stowed away between her mattress and the wall, or orange peels growing green beards in a bowl shoved under her bed. The floor in her room was a carpet of anything and everything she had touched, played with, read, or worn since the last time my mom had made her tidy up in there. I was the first off of the diving board; she wouldn't even try. She was lactose intolerant, but nobody said anything like that back then, so her nose ran constantly. She sometimes still peed the bed and wasn't interested in what my dad was building in the shop. Sometimes at school it was hard to tell which of us was pretending not to know who the other one was most convincingly.

Christopher was a little less than a year younger than Carrie, my mom's little sister Roberta's eldest son. He was scrawny and awkward, built a little like a preying mantis crossed with a little boy. All right angles and pointy bits, he was prone to tripping over his own feet and walking into his own booby-traps. He liked guns and tanks and knives and slingshots and matches and should never, ever have been trusted with any of those things. He got picked on mercilessly in school the minute any of the rest of us turned our back even for a second.

Danny was my favourite. Round and sunburned and nearly always smiling, he loved to draw and paint and had an imaginary dragon as his best friend. He would politely tug on the skirt of a lady my Gran was chatting with at the supermarket to inform her that she was accidentally standing on his dragon's tail, and if she wouldn't mind moving a little to the right? One whole summer he pretended to be a dog, and my aunt Robbie just humoured him and played along whenever my gran wasn't home. Gran claimed that crawling about on all fours was wearing out the knees of his trousers too soon and it would cost us an arm and a leg to keep him looking decent if we let him keep up with that being a dog nonsense.

As much as we all bickered and pushed and shoved each other all the time, and fought over who got which piece of cake or pie or who ate the last of the raspberry jam and put the empty jar back into the fridge, I think we managed to love each other pretty good back then. But my default on the surface emotion was mostly hating having to look after them, until someone else threatened or hurt one of them, and then a fierce and protective surge of red hot blood would flood into my chest and thrum past my eardrums, curling my hands into fists.

Nanaimo felt and smelled like a big city to us Yukon kids: we could find all kinds of radio stations on my little transistor radio, and we only had two stations back home. There were huge-to-us shopping malls off of the four-lane highway, and the buses ran on Sundays, too. Pee-yew, we would yell and hold our noses and reel around on the front sidewalk on muggy mornings when the rotten egg smell of the pulp mill hung everywhere in the air all around us. Our gran would cluck her tongue and shake her head at us and say, "You smell that? That's the smell of a good union job, that is what that is. You should be so lucky to grow up and get yourself a good job at the mill. Pay all your bills and then some. You're spoiled, the lot of yous."

We had all arrived in Nanaimo via a four-day Greyhound bus ride, fueled by wax-paper-wrapped ham and cheese sandwiches and warm juice boxes and lots of I spy with my naked eye games and sweaty crayons and supermarket colouring books and sporadic bouts of sleeping that left us whining about kinks in our necks. "Get off the bus then, and run around for a bit. Stretch your legs," Gran told us in Fort Nelson and Fort St. John and Prince George and Cache Creek, and the pine trees grew fatter and taller and the air more humid as we bumped our dusty way south.

My gran had sent all of her furniture and dishes and belongings down the Alaska Highway via a Ryder moving truck, scheduling it all so the truck was supposed to arrive the day after we did. But that truck had jackknifed while braking to avoid a bull moose somewhere just north of Dawson Creek and tipped onto its side, scattering boxes and smashing enough of her stuff that delivery was delayed for several weeks while the moving company sorted through everything and decided what the damages were going to be worth.

It must have been hellish for her, rattling around her empty house with four kids and without so much as a spoon or a bowl or her infamous cast-iron pans, but I remember that time as being kind of an extended adventure, like we were camping out on the carpet in the living room for three weeks. She instructed us to stuff all of our long pants and sweaters into pillowcases she bought us at the Sally Ann to devise makeshift pillows, and to spread our sleeping bags out like mattresses and sleep sprawled in a row under just a second-hand sheet. My sheet had Smokey the Bear on it and I loved it. It had "Only You Can Prevent Forest Fires" printed all over it, and Smokey was wearing overalls and had a shovel in one paw and a robin perched on one shoulder. We got it from the hospital thrift store for a quarter.

My gran let us do things during this camping-in-the-house period that she never would have let us do if we had furniture and dishes, such as eat cereal out of those individual tiny boxes with the perforated lines where you opened them up like little square cardboard bowls. She said it was highway robbery, what they charged her for them, and we would fight over who got the Sugar Corn Pops or the Froot Loops and who had to eat the Raisin Bran. We would sit cross-legged in a circle where she planned to put her kitchen table when it finally arrived, and wolf down hot dogs and canned beans with plastic cutlery she told us to grab from the 7-Eleven when she bought us all Coke Slurpees. We listened to classic rock on my transistor radio and danced the jitterbug in the kitchen like our moms did when the Beatles first came here and she never once complained about having to buy new batteries for it.

I remember feeling a sad little tug in my chest when the moving truck finally arrived and the sweating men carried the furniture and television and boxes up the stairs and into the living room and kitchen, my grandmother hovering around them saying what went where and telling them to mind the new paint and wipe their boots. Sure, we had real pillows and bunk beds now. But it was Raisin Bran for everyone, and we weren't allowed to read with our flashlights under the covers anymore like we were camping. Plus I had to vacuum now that we had a vacuum again and we all had to be quiet when my gran's shows or the news came on the television.

It was all over the news that summer, about the missing kids in Vancouver. Eleven of them, by the time we got the furniture at the end of July and started watching the news again. Sometimes Gran would scoot my sister and cousins out of the living room and make them go play Memory or Battleship or Operation in the bedroom while we watched the six o'clock news alone.

She would cluck her tongue and cross herself. "You can never be too careful out there," she would tell me over and over. "You're the oldest. You're responsible. Don't you ever let them out of your sight for a minute, d'you hear me?" She would point her index finger at me, which was curled into a comma by her arthritis already, and shake her head at the state of the world. "Because God forbid anything should happen to any of yous while I'm responsible. Your poor mothers. I'd never forgive meself. I just wouldn't."

I took this responsibility as seriously as I could, considering I was almost twelve and only sixteen months older than my little sister Carrie and she would never do anything I told her to, nearly ever, and Christopher and Dan were like two little monkeys, climbing over each other and everything and eating plants we didn't know the names for just to see what they tasted like, and falling out of trees and off of fences on the regular.

I tried telling them one morning when we were hanging the laundry and watering the freshly seeded vegetable garden that they had to listen to me more, that we had to stick together because there was a killer on the loose and kids were disappearing and if anything happened, well, think of our poor mothers, God forbid, right? But Carrie rolled her eyes at me and Christopher picked at a scab on his knee and Dan licked the dry snot under his nostril. It was no use. They were too little. It was up to me to make sure that killer never got one of us.

We spent the better part of any day that wasn't pouring rain outside picking apples and plums and cherries and pears that were not quite ripe yet, with northern kid amazement at the bounty all around us, and eating them until we felt sick, and walking miles every day along the shoulder of the road to the reservoir so we could swim and laze around on threadbare beach towels on the patchy grass next to the water. We would search the bulrushes and long grass in the ditch next to the road for discarded pop and beer bottles that we could trade in at the corner store for money to buy gumballs and Lik-M-Aid sticks and popsicles with.

We walked nearly everywhere. There and back, to the mall for groceries, to the garden store, to the food co-op for cases of canned tomato soup and bags of rice. If it was just us kids, I would go first, then my sister, then the two boys, straggling along behind us like filthy ducklings. If Gran was with us it was more of a forced march, usually her up front holding Carrie's hand, and me right behind towing Chris and Dan. She had little tolerance for what she called dilly-dallying.

But that warm July night, the crickets were singing and a cool breeze was rippling in the long grass next to the road, and lawn sprinklers were thrumming on front lawns and my gran said she could smell the lavender blooming and it reminded her of England when she and some girls from the factory where she used to work got to visit the countryside that one summer before the war.

So we slowed down.

I dropped each of the boys' sweaty little paws and we meandered, smelling flowers and pulling stems of grass so we could eat the pale sweet shoots, and, as always, keeping our eyes peeled for the nickel-each gleam of discarded bottles in the ditches and culverts.

I took my eyes off of the boys, and I forgot to keep up with my gran and my sister too. A truck drove by a little too close to the shoulder of the road, startling me, and I jumped back and instinctively held my arms wide to herd my cousins further off the road. I looked up to see if my grandmother had witnessed this close call, but she and my little sister were gone. They had turned off the main road somewhere, and I had not been paying close enough attention and had failed to follow them. I jogged back to the last intersection, looked both ways. Couldn't see them anywhere. Jogged back to where my cousins were standing, scratching their bug bites and kicking the dirt.

My heart started to pound in my throat a little. I grabbed one of each of the boys' hands again.

"I didn't see where Gran and Carrie turned off. Did you guys?" I asked, trying not to let any fear seep into my voice.

They shook their heads in perfect tandem. Christopher needed a haircut and Danny had an orangeish Slurpee stain all the way around his mouth. They suddenly looked younger than they had a minute ago, long lashes brushing across big wet eyes.

"Nobody needs to freak out, okay, we aren't that lost. We just need to walk around a bit, until we see something that looks familiar."

But nothing looked familiar. We had been walking home from looking at a used bedroom set that my gran had found for sale in the newspaper in a part of the neighbourhood we had never been to before, and the older man who was selling the furniture had told my grandmother about a shorter way to walk home than the route we had taken there. He had sketched her a little map on a scrap of paper, but I hadn't been paying attention because the house next door had a cardboard box of newborn kittens in the garage and the neighbours had let all four of us file in and watch them sleeping, curled up into their mother's belly. I had no idea where we were, and only a vague idea of which way home was.

I knew we lived at number 10 Rosamond Street, but I didn't know where Rosamond Street was. We didn't have a phone hooked up yet, mostly because the phone itself had just arrived with the rest of the furniture a couple of days ago. I sat down on a large rock parked next to a stop sign to think it over.

I needed to find a gas station or a little old lady out weeding or watering her lawn and ask for directions. Those were my two safest options, the way I figured it. Little old ladies might be most likely to give you a lecture about walking on their grass or did our mothers know where we were, but I had never heard of one abducting and murdering children. And gas station guys were used to giving directions, and at least I knew the guy had a decent job.

We wandered around for about half an hour, the sun starting to dip dangerously close to dusk in the sky, and none of the streets or houses looked friendly or familiar. No gas stations. No corner stores. We slunk past an elementary school, the windows shuttered like eyelids and the playground abandoned, the chains on the swing set creaking when the wind gusted up.

Everything started feeling scary in that quiet orange evening light. A shirtless man was watering the shrubs next to his driveway with a green hose, but he had full, dark, hooded eyebrows and a bleeding tattoo of a skull on his shoulder, so I hurried my cousins past his house without making eye contact. I didn't know what a child murderer looked like, but I wasn't about to take any chances.

The road splintered off to the left into the mouth of a well-tended trailer park, and the second trailer in had a Block Parent sign scotch-taped into the front bay window. The trailer had a fresh coat of pale yellow paint on it, and flower boxes dripping with lobelia and baby's breath hung from the railing on the deck. The little lawn was freshly mowed.

I remembered the whole Block Parent thing from an assembly we had in the school gymnasium when I was in grade four. Block Parent signs were supposed to mark houses where you could go if you got lost or were in danger. The people inside might be strangers, but they were supposed to be of the safe variety. I had been unconvinced that day in the school gymnasium, and I was still skeptical now.

The way I figured it was, if I were the type of person who was into stealing children, then I would put a Block Parent sign in my window. What could be easier, and who would ever think to look in the house with the Block Parent sign in the window? You wouldn't even have to go to all the trouble of going out and finding a child to snatch, you could just sit around on the couch and watch TV and wait for a lost kid to come knocking.

I turned to Christopher and put my hands on both of his shoulders. Made him look me right in the eye.

"You see that trailer, right there? Number eleven? I'm going to go and knock on the door and see if I can get some directions on how to get us home, okay?"

He nodded solemnly.

"But I don't know the people inside, so I'm taking your brother with me, but I want you to stay right here. Don't move, okay? And if we don't come out in like, five minutes, I need you to go and find an adult and call the police, okay? Tell them we were last seen going into trailer number eleven and he has probably got us."

"Who is he?"

I took a deep breath, looked right, looked left. "You don't need to know. You're still too little. Which trailer?"

"Trailer number eleven."

"Don't move. Stay right here. You got me?"

He nodded.

I walked up the four stairs and rapped on the door, dragging Danny with me.

A woman in a fading flowered housedress opened the inside door and squinted through the screen door at us. I cleared my throat, stood up straighter.

"Uh ... sorry to bother you, ma'am, but I saw the Block Parent sign and we just moved here and I don't know my way around so good yet, and I was supposed to be paying attention but I guess I looked down for too long and I lost my gran and my sister and I know we live on Rosamond Street but I don't know where that street is, and our phone isn't hooked up yet so I can't call and there's no gas stations around here that I can find and I am the oldest and I should have been ..."

She let out a crusty little chuckle and held up one hand to signal that I could stop talking. So I did.

"You poor little things. Rosamond Street, you say? You're not too far from there. Let me rouse old Reggie off of the couch and he can drive you both home. Your poor grandmother. I bet she's beside herself."

She swung the screen door open with a loose-skinned arm and motioned for us to come in. Danny followed her pointed finger and stepped into the kitchen. It smelled like boiling corn on the cob in there.

"Thank you very much. I just have to go get my other cousin. I left him on the road outside just in case you were ..."

She raised one eyebrow.

"Um ... not home." I looked down so she could not see my lie so easily, and turned on one heel to scurry back across the deck and down the stairs.

But Christopher was gone. I could see for at least a block in either direction, and there was no flash of red and yellow striped t-shirt, no brown corduroy shorts, no filthy running shoes or scrawny scabby little legs pumping. No cousin. Gone.

The lady told us her name was Annie, and this was her husband Reggie. She told me not to panic and to drink this glass of water. She gave Danny a chocolate-covered digestive cookie and told Reggie to start the car. She was going to get on the horn she said, and get the phone tree happening. We would have him home in no time, she promised, we all just needed to keep our heads.

Reggie let me ride up front, and Danny pouted from the back seat. I felt annoyed with him that he would even care about something like who got to sit where when his own brother was missing when there was a murderer on the loose and anything could happen.

It was nearly dark when Reggie's headlights scrolled across the cedar hedge in front of number ten Rosamond Street. I could see the shape of my grandmother in our house from the driveway, her one hand held like a brim over her eyes so she could peer through the living room window at us. She paced back and forth, and then the silhouette of her appeared behind the pebbled glass window in the front door. She opened it wide just as Reggie was reaching for the doorbell. He dropped his hand back to his side.

"Looks like these two got a little turned around." He placed a wide hard palm on my shoulder. "Your oldest here, she saw we were Block Parents and knocked to ask for directions. Smart kid. Your other boy was waiting on the street and must have got spooked and run off. My wife is at home rustling up a bunch of folks from our temple to get a search party together. We'll track him down, don't you worry now. He can't have got too far. Oh, and my name is Reggie. Reggie Cluff. I should mention that."

My gran grabbed me by one hand and dragged me into the front hallway. She pulled Danny by the neck of his t-shirt, and he wrapped both of his chubby arms around her one thigh.

"I can't thank you enough, Mr. Cluff. I'm just worried sick. I was about to go next door and call the police. We just moved here and they haven't come to hook the phone up yet. And where is Christopher?" Her eyes on me like two laser beams. "What am I always telling you about dilly-dallying around? You see? You see what happens? You better pray he gets home safe and sound, you."

"We should all pray," Reggie said, and my grandmother immediately made the sign of the cross in the air in front of her, and I followed. Reggie did not. He crossed his arms and bowed his head. Danny started to cry, and my gran didn't tell him to stop.

My grandmother was a proud woman, never one to ask for or accept help from anyone, ever. But in the next fifteen minutes or so, about thirty strangers arrived and parked their trucks and cars all up and down our little gravel street and gathered on our lawn, flashlights bobbing in the long summer dusk.

A map was spread out on the ticking hood of a Toyota pick-up truck and search areas were assigned. A police cruiser arrived too, and two officers got out and stretched their backs, wrote things down in their books, spoke into their squawking radios. Neighbours started to trickle out onto front stoops to see what was going on. My grandmother hovered on the perimeter, her cheeks flushed and her skin stretched tight over the bones in her face. I was in big trouble, I could tell. The kind of trouble so big it would have to wait for later.

The men gathered in a circle like a football huddle and said a quick prayer. "In the name of Jesus Christ, amen." Reggie finished up and they all headed to their vehicles.

"These people are all Mormons," my grandmother hissed at me like this was somehow all my fault too.

They brought Christopher home in the back of a squad car, wrapped in a grey flannel blanket, nearly two hours later. A man named Eric had spotted him bolting along the shoulder of the road several miles from Annie and Reggie's trailer park, his fists and knees pumping in a terrified race to nowhere at all. One leg of his shorts was ripped into three ribbons and his face and arms and legs were bleeding from a hundred different bramble scratches. Christopher had refused to stop running when Eric had slowed the car down next to him, just kept straight on, full speed, eyes fixed on the horizon. Eric had been forced to pull over, jump out, and tackle the terrified little boy to the ground to get him to stop.

"That is right about when he peed his pants, poor little guy." Eric recounted the story to the folks standing in a circle in our driveway, and everyone laughed. Everyone but my grandmother and me.

For the rest of that summer, the Mormons dropped in to check on us. Reggie would show up with a weed whacker and his lawn mower bumping around in the hatchback of his station wagon, and do our lawn. Eric came by with a small blue bicycle for us all to share, his son had outgrown it, he said. My grandmother was always reserved and polite. She would thank them too many times and offer them crumpled up bills from her wallet, which they refused. As soon as they were gone, she would narrow her eyes at me.

I asked her one time why Catholics like us weren't supposed to get along with the Mormons. "Was it because they came to your front door without being invited?"

"Well, there is that," she confessed. "No one should go about telling people what to believe, it's just wrong. But worse than that is, they believe they're the only ones who will get to go to heaven." She set her knitting down to look at me, to see if the gravity of this had registered on my face properly.

I wrinkled my nose. "But isn't that what we believe too?"

"Go outside and water the garden," she told me. "Don't make me tell you twice."

There was a drought that summer, and every morning after the news about how the police were confident they were making headway on the case of the missing children in the Vancouver area, the weatherman would announce how many days it had been since there had been any precipitation. Fifty-six days, the weatherman said, in the middle of the last week of July.

Then it happened. I felt the air change around me one night when I was bringing in the laundry. There was a new smell in my nostrils, heavy and earthy, like fresh topsoil, and the wind picked up and left goose pimples on my arms as I unpinned the sheets and towels and folded them into the wicker basket.

The first rumble of thunder came as the four of us were playing Monopoly in a circle on the carpet in the living room and my gran was knitting on the couch. The neighbour's dog started to howl plaintively, and my gran clucked her tongue. "Foolish old hound," she tutted, her needles clicking together. Then the rain followed, hard and fast and on an angle, bouncing back off of the pavement into itself and hammering on the tin roof of our garden shed. It didn't rain like that in the Yukon, and we jumped up and pressed our noses to the living room window to watch it come down.

"Can we go play in it?" someone asked and Gran said "Yes, but in bare feet or wear your flip-flops so you don't ruin your shoes and socks."

The rain was warm and falling so hard it drummed audibly on the leaves of the apple trees and the big cedar. The ground was parched and dry and the street in front of our house was a mess of little rivers immediately. Lightning flashes lit the world up in blinding colour a couple of times a minute, and we all froze, unsure of how scared we should be. I tried to remember what they had told us in school during the safety assembly about lightning. Were we supposed to stand in a doorway, or was that in case of an earthquake? Stand under a big tree or avoid trees altogether?

I shook danger out of my head and danced around on the lawn with my little sister and my cousins. Then Gran appeared on the front porch.

"Get back in here before you get zapped like little bugs. Mind you don't tear up the wet grass," she said. "And strip out of those wet clothes and hang them on the rack in the laundry room." Her words were stern, but she was smiling.

We had a hard time getting to sleep that night, the rain pelting and rolling down the window in our bedroom, and lightning strikes flash-capturing our naked legs on top of the covers and leaving bleached spots behind our eyelids when we closed them.

It was still raining when we woke up, and Gran announced she was going to go to mass that morning and then to get the groceries by herself.

"You lot can stay in this morning and amuse yourselves on your own." She shot a look in my direction that I knew meant I was in charge of making sure we stayed out of trouble. "If I'm not back by lunchtime then you can heat up some soup and fix yourselves a nice sandwich."

I was going to be twelve in less than two weeks. I was in charge of anything that involved the stove or the washer and dryer; even the toaster was off-limits to my little sister and cousins. This was one rare area where my authority was never questioned by the younger kids; Christopher had a thick veiny pale patch of scar tissue on part of his chest and under his arm from where he had pulled a pot of boiling water down on himself when he was just a toddler. The nobody-but-me-touches-the-stove rule was sacred, and went unchallenged.

We did the dishes and swept the kitchen. We made our beds and put the Legos away. Then we stretched out on the couch and the carpet and listened to Beatles records for a bit, then Supertramp's *Breakfast in America*, and read paperbacks and comic books. Finally we turned the television on.

We could get four channels if you played with the rabbit ears on top of the set for a little bit, but the same thing was on all four channels. Princess Diana was marrying Prince Charles over in England; it had been on the radio all morning too. Even the stations that usually just played all the hits all the time were talking about the stupid Royal stupid Wedding.

I could not have imagined anything more boring to watch on television than two people getting married, even two famous royal people, but there was nothing else on. It took nearly an hour for the motorcade to even arrive at the church. We all sighed and poked each other and argued about whose turn it was to lie on the couch all by themself.

Finally Princess Diana entered the church, her golden hair perfectly coiffed around her rosy-cheeked face and her white gown trailing behind her. Charles looking all Adam's-apple-and-hair-grease in his uniform and polished medals and epaulets. I could see why my dad hated it so much when people said they sort of looked alike. *What an arsehole,* I could hear him saying in my head. Not that my father would ever watch the royal wedding, no matter how hard it was raining or how bored he was.

The announcer lowered his voice reverently as the princess slowly walked up the aisle. "Look at her, ladies and gentleman, every inch a royal princess, in every sense of the word. How beautiful. Every little girl in the whole world wants to be just like her today. Every little girl in the whole wide world."

Those words shot out of the tinny speaker in my grandmother's old cabinet television and pierced through the skin of my still flat chest like poisoned darts. I didn't want a dress like that, a dress so long other people had to follow you around and carry it for you. I didn't want my hair and makeup to be perfect so I could marry some chinless British guy who didn't even earn his own war medals.

My little sister was staring at the television screen, transfixed. It's hard for me to find words for the kind of lonely I felt in my belly, in my whole body, in that moment. Felt like lead in the blood in my veins, so heavy it held me down from the inside of me.

I knew already that I wasn't like most little girls. I didn't like the things they liked and I didn't get how or why to play Barbies and I mostly stayed away from large groups of girls at school. I was scared of the way they whispered in each other's ears and I hated gymnastics and volleyball, too. I was well used to being excluded from their unspoken cliques and only got invited to their birthday parties if our mothers knew each other from working in the same office. I knew I was different and most of the time I was okay with that.

What I didn't realize until that moment was that I was the only little girl like me in the whole wide world.

On August 11, I turned twelve years old. We had my favourite spaghetti and meat balls for dinner and an ice cream cake from Dairy Queen with Woody the Woodpecker on it stuttering happy birthday in translucent blue icing.

On August 12, serial killer Clifford Olson was arrested outside of Nanaimo, a short car ride from our front door. He had just picked up two female hitchhikers in a rented car.

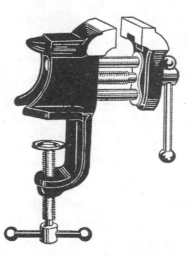

SMALL BENCH VISE

The vise is used to hold metal parts while they are bent, drilled, filed, sawed, etc.

# A DARK BLUE BIKE

The summer right before I started grade seven I got a new bike. A blue ten-speed with curled handlebars wrapped in white plastic tape and hand brakes. My old bike had been a purple one-speed with a sparkly banana seat. I had never loved it.

My dad drove us back with my brand new bike in the back of his old red Ford truck. Once we got home, he lifted it out of the back of the truck easily with one arm and set it down on the driveway. Then he lifted the back tire up off the ground and spun it with two fingers. It made a very pleasing clicking noise.

"You sure you know how to work the gears on this thing?" He was squinting at me, a smoldering cigarette dangling in one corner of his mouth. "It's a bit more complicated than your old one, you know. Way easier for the chain to fall off on these ones, too."

"Jenny Bailey lets me ride hers all the time," I lied. She would barely let any of us even look at her new bike.

He shrugged and watched me clamber onto the bike seat and coast down our driveway.

I pedaled slowly in too high of a gear along our street and ended up having to dismount and push the bike up the hill in the middle of Twelfth Avenue. But speeding down the other side was no problem, my short hair blowing back away from my face and the wind pulling tears out of the corners of my eyes. I pedaled as hard as I could from the bottom of the hill all the way to the turn-off onto Hickory Street at the top of Mountainview Drive.

I experimented with one gearshift, and then the other, and

heard the gears grinding near my back tire. The bike shuddered and the mechanism that I would soon discover was called the derailleur skipped back and forth to accommodate my inexperienced shifting. I pedaled with my head bent, eyes down, watching the chain slide

from one sprocket to another and back, starting to see how everything worked.

Next thing I knew I was blinking my eyes and trying to get them to focus. Everything was upside down and spinning, and my mouth tasted like dirty pennies. I stared straight ahead, trying to understand what my eyes were telling me I was looking at. A curb. A black truck tire. A bumper with a muddy licence plate bolted to it. Blood. My blood.

Blood all over my shirt, pumping still out of my nose and onto the dusty road under me. I sat up and put my head back, pinched the bridge of my nose like they taught us to do in softball when you caught a line drive with your face.

I had apparently pedaled my bike straight into a parked truck, and its back canopy window was a maze of cracks. I wasn't sure if those cracks were from the crown of my pounding head or not, but I wasn't going to stick around to find out.

I stood my new bike up and brushed the dirt and gravel off of my jeans and hopped on, standing up on the pedals so I could race away as fast as I could.

But my bike chain had fallen off, and my front rim was bent enough to bring upon a serious wobble, and when I pedaled hard the lack of resistance sent me sailing over my own scraped handle-bars and I bit the pavement again, this time palms and chin first. A dog started to bark from behind the living room window of the house that the damaged truck was parked in front of.

I cried all the way home, pushing my broken bike and choking on tears and blood and dirt and snot. My dad was in the front yard, dragging the sprinkler across the grass, another smoke dangling. Or maybe it was the same cigarette? I had been gone a total of about seven minutes.

I thought he would be mad about my damaged bike, but he didn't say a thing about that. He just smiled with one side of his mouth and asked if I was I missing any teeth.

"No," I said, touching each one of them with my bloody tongue. I had stopped crying as soon as I saw him. Crying made him ner-vous for some reason. He tolerated it from my little sister, but not so much from me.

He held my chin between his greasy thumb and forefinger, and squinted down his nose at me, turning my face to the right, and then the left.

"Go clean yourself up before your mom gets home from her night school," he said. "Spray that stain cleaner stuff on that shirt and put it all in the washer right now. I can fix your bike."

If we were a hugging kind of family I would have hugged him, but we weren't, so it didn't cross my mind.

# I SHINE MY ARMOUR EVERY NIGHT

My best friend from grade two until about grade ten was named Janine Jones. She had freckles and big front teeth and two brothers, a mean older one named Jerome and a mostly useless younger one named Marcus. Her brown hair was much thicker than mine, she would say, which is why she needed to use conditioner but I didn't.

Her parents were Catholic like my family was, so we never had to explain any of that to each other, and we liked most of the same things. We were both into books: Nancy Drew, Harriet the Spy, Encyclopedia Brown, and later, anything with even a passing mention of sex in it: Judy Blume's *Are You There God, It's Me, Margaret*, and those *Clan of the Cave Bear* books, the whole *Flowers in the Attic* series. But mostly we were obsessed with a book called *The Chrysalids*.

We spent a lot of time lying on our backs on the side lawn of her house on Pine Street, before the new subdivision went in when her street was still quiet, wishing we had been born special with extra toes, and practicing our powers of telepathy. I would think of a colour and imagine it in my head. She would try to mind-meld with me and see if she could see the colour and name it. We did the same thing with numbers and playing cards, guessing over and over until one of us got it right and then rolling around on the grass laughing, convinced that our supernatural powers were growing stronger.

I would check my oversized wristwatch repeatedly to see if it was 4:30 yet. That was when we had to split up; she would head back into her house to start dinner and make her and her brother's lunches, and I had to ride my bike home and put the Shake 'N Bake chicken in the oven or pour the can of mushroom soup over the pork chops and put the rice on.

It was what we did. Weekend nights we would sleep in a tent in her back yard, and record giggling broadcasts for the radio show we were going to have one day, pretend-interviewing each other being the guy who rescued ten people from a burning apartment building or the first woman to walk on the moon or a farmer who broke the Guinness World Record for growing the biggest squash.

When we started band class in grade eight, she picked the clarinet and I settled on playing the alto saxophone, because there were too many boys who signed up to play the drums already. We would practice every night, playing "Billie Jean" by Michael Jackson and "Boogie Woogie Bugle Boy" faster and faster until she would squeak a fart out from blowing so hard and I would fall off my chair laughing.

And then late that September David Altman asked her to go to the nine o'clock late show of *The Empire Strikes Back* with him. The late show. On a Friday night. Janine said yes and bought light blue eye shadow at Shoppers Drug Mart and started wearing it immediately.

She borrowed her mom's pink Daisy Razor and nicked the freckled skin on her legs in six different places. Started talking about getting a pair of grey tights to go with the dress she wore to her uncle's wedding in Alberta. Asked her mom if she could get another spiral perm.

I felt a strange combination of jealousy and disgust every time she crooned David Altman's name or wrote it on the front of her binder in purple ballpoint pen with a heart for the dot over the i. I didn't want to take her to the movies and tongue kiss in the second to last row from the back while Luke Skywalker blew up the Death Star. It wasn't that kind of jealousy. It was more like I just didn't want her to want to go with him so much. None of the boys at school ever noticed me like that; it was like they looked straight over me to Tracy Darling or Wendy Buss or Sandra Chounaird. Those girls and their tinkling laughs and mascara-draped eyes, the way they lowered their lids halfway and not quite stared back at those boys. The way their pink angora sweaters hugged the bumpy little beginnings of their chests and rode up over their flat bellies when they reached for something on the top shelf of their lockers. The way they snapped their gum and whispered the important stuff and said everything else that didn't matter loud enough for everyone to hear them.

If Janine Jones was going to start acting like the rest of them then I was going to have to find a new best friend because none of that type of business came naturally to me at all.

It was nearing the end of September and Janine's whole back yard smelled like poplar sap and pine needles in the late afternoon sun. The poplar and willow and birch leaves had turned bright yellow and pylon orange but hadn't fallen; one good wind and they would be all over the grass, but they weren't yet. They looked so postcard bright, framed by the deep dark green of the pine trees and the dusty green of the spruce, and not a cloud in a perfect blue sky. The Macleods' stupid standard poodle was barking at nothing as usual across the street. The soft whup whup of a sprinkler from the yard next door.

We were reading and eating popcorn from a bowl on the grass between us, stretched out on our backs on an old baby blue wool blanket with soft satin trim. It smelled like the floor of a tent in the sunshine.

Janine rolled on her side and looked at me, blowing her newly curled bangs out of her eyes.

"I'm going to the movies with David this Friday. The late show."

I rolled my eyes. "No duh. It's practically the only thing you've talked about for like two weeks already."

"I have an idea," she said, ignoring my lack of enthusiasm for her romantic life. She propped herself up on one elbow and leaned over me, her face only a couple of inches from mine. I could smell popcorn and cherry lip-gloss.

"You want to sneak downstairs and see if we can catch Jerome whacking off again? It's four-oh-three p.m., after all."

Janine laughed and shook her head. "Father Mickey made him say so many Hail Marys last week after mass, the rest of us had to wait in the car for him for twenty minutes. But no. Different idea."

I shrugged.

"I think you and I should practice kissing," she said. "Together. Like, not for real, just to build up our skills. French kissing. David went out with Michelle Richards for all of last winter. She went to Whitehorse Elementary before she moved to Porter Creek. You know what those girls are like. I'm going to need to practice. You'll have to learn too, you know, sometime, right? You can't just stick your tongue down a guy's throat. You need to learn a technique for it."

I have thought a lot about this moment in the many years since, flipped these few minutes over and studied their underbelly. Asked myself all the questions I could come up with. I was never in love with my best friend Janine. I never stared at her body when we were swimming or getting changed, I wasn't attracted to her in that way, ever. I only looked at her body to compare it to mine, which I always found lacking somehow. I was skinnier than her. I was paler. My chest was flat. So was my ass. I didn't like my body much, but I didn't desire hers either. I had sexual fantasies, but they were less to do with body parts of any particular gender and more to do with what I recognize now was my burgeoning kinkiness: I jerked off while thinking about that scene from *Planet of the Apes* where Charlton Heston is wearing a collar attached to wrist restraints and a dirty loincloth and he has to stand there in front of a tribunal of orangutans in leather and try to convince them that he is in fact a cultured man from another planet who can speak. Or the part where the gorillas chase him on horseback with bullwhips. Or when they catch him in a rope net. Needless to say, I kept these details to myself.

I have wondered many times about why I did what happened next, and what fueled the fear that curled up cold from out of my belly and made me jump to my feet. I can't remember if I mumbled an excuse or an apology or if I said anything at all.

I only remember leaping on my new bike and pedaling home as fast as I could. I remember barely stopping to lean my bike up against a post in the carport and fumbling to get the front door open. I kicked off my shoes and bolted through the kitchen and upstairs into my bedroom and slammed the door behind me.

Then I let the tears flood over my bottom lids and down my face. The hot, burning kind that make you make a sound in your chest you don't recognize as your own, a sound that catches at the top of your throat and tears a hole there before it escapes your mouth.

I didn't want to kiss my friend. Her lips were puffy and covered in butter and I didn't know how we would look at each other after, or what we would say, but that wasn't it. That wasn't what I was crying about. I wouldn't know for six more years what was still stuffed way down inside of me that scared me so much.

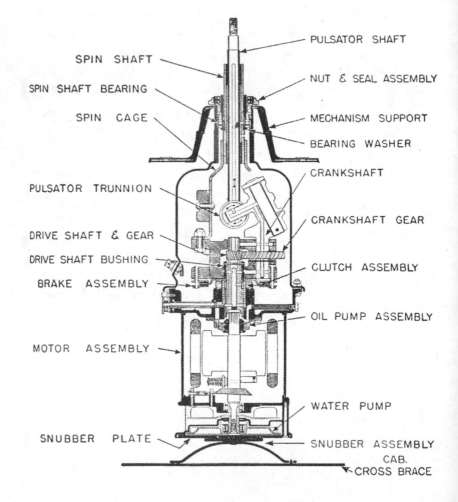

SPIN SHAFT

SPIN SHAFT BEARING

SPIN CAGE

PULSATOR TRUNNION

DRIVE SHAFT & GEAR

DRIVE SHAFT BUSHING

BRAKE ASSEMBLY

MOTOR ASSEMBLY

SNUBBER PLATE

PULSATOR SHAFT

NUT & SEAL ASSEMBLY

MECHANISM SUPPORT

BEARING WASHER

CRANKSHAFT

CRANKSHAFT GEAR

CLUTCH ASSEMBLY

OIL PUMP ASSEMBLY

WATER PUMP

SNUBBER ASSEMBLY
CAB.
CROSS BRACE

# I BELIEVE YOU

My Rob Brezsny horoscope for this week, the week of my forty-sixth birthday, reads as follows:

"What are the best things and the worst things in your life, and when are you going to get around to whispering or shouting them?" This question was posed by Leo author Ray Bradbury in his book *Zen in the Art of Writing: Essays on Creativity*. Even if you're not a writer yourself, you will benefit from responding to his exhortation. It's one of the best things you could possibly do to activate your dormant creativity and intensify your lust for life. This is one of those times when working with your extremes is not only safe and healthy, but also fun and inspirational. So do it, Leo! Get excited and expressive about the best and worst things in your life."

So. I'm going to write about one of the things that scares me the most to write about. How do I not write like a victim? Will he sue me if I write about what happened? It was so long ago, maybe I should just leave it be? I'm going to reassure myself with the fact that if the guy I am about to write about sues me for libel, it would mean him admitting that he is the guy I am writing about. He has some kind of a job in politics now, I'm not sure what, since I try not to know much about him. Hopefully just the threat of a scandal will keep me safe. I already know that he is not a good man.

When the Jian Ghomeshi scandal broke last year, the case where the popular and handsome-to-some national CBC radio personality came under the spotlight after years of rumours and investigations by journalists for numerous assaults on multiple women, I found myself having an unexpectedly strong reaction every time anyone I knew insisted that we wait until the guy had his proper say in court before we found him guilty.

I got into a fight on the phone with one of my favourite cousins about it, in fact. My position was that we always wait for justice but it rarely comes, and in the meanwhile, predators continue with business as usual. I told my cousin that every time he said on Facebook that Ghomeshi was innocent until proven guilty he was telling all the women in his life—his wife, his daughter, his nieces, his mother, his female friends and co-workers—that he is not the guy to tell if they are raped or assaulted or sexually harassed. That he is not a safe harbour. Not a confidant, and not in their corner.

At first I couldn't figure out why every time I read another article supporting or calling for patience or facts or more proof against Jian, or Cosby, or Woody Allen, the tears welled up so hot and easy, why my stomach knotted itself into itself and wouldn't come undone for hours after.

Then it came over me in the shower one morning. The stream of hot water burped a little and turned cold for a few seconds when one of my neighbours turned their dishwasher or washing machine on, and the truth jumped into my chest like a frozen boulder and stayed there, making it hard to breathe or think about anything else.

I was date-raped in grade ten by a popular boy at school. Let's say his name was Kevin and he was a basketball player. Neither of these things are true, but let's say them anyway. Let's protect him even to this day, because this is what we do. We protect him as a means of surviving ourselves.

He was in grade twelve. He had a group of friends, the definition of a clique, who were athletes and got good grades and were handsome and all going to university. They drove their own cars to school and had new sweaters and backpacks for the first day of classes.

I don't know why he asked me out. I was two years younger, I had no boobs and hung out with a different crowd, and my friends had all come to the only high school in town together from the junior high in Porter Creek. Maybe it was because we both played the saxophone? Or maybe he played the trombone, but I'm hiding the truth in here somewhere so I can write down what really happened. I don't know. We didn't date for very long.

His parents worked out of town a lot, and his older sister was away going to school somewhere down south. He often had the house to himself, which was unusual. He would never let his friends talk him into big crazy my-parents-are-away-for-the-weekend parties like some kids threw though, he was too smart for that.

It was winter, and cold. Maybe early December? I can't remember the details now, just that it was cold and dark. Snowing a little. We were in his basement in the rec room, on an old couch. He wanted me to give him a blowjob, but I was freaked out. His dick was pushing at the buttons on his Levi's 501 jeans, and he popped the buttons open and pulled his underwear down and took it out. It was crooked. I remember thinking it was crooked, and was that normal? It was the first hard penis I had seen in real life up close.

"Just put it in your mouth," he said. I don't remember if I ever said yes or not. What I do remember was him on top of me then, me on my back on that old orange and brown and mustard coloured plaid couch and his dick all the way inside my mouth and down my throat and gagging and pushing him off me and spitting it all out and then bolting up the stairs to the front door and grabbing my parka and snow boots and running down the sidewalk in the cold and white and silence of a Yukon winter.

I heard him behind me, swearing and calling me a bitch, and starting his car, the engine gunning as he backed up down the driveway and then drove off. I ran, the frigid air feeling clean and burning my nostrils and the back of my throat. Ducked into an alley and squatted down behind a little frame that held two old garbage cans. His headlights scrolled the garage door above me and then kept on driving. I could hear the tires on his hand-me-down-from-Daddy car squeaking on the fresh snow as he drove slowly past the alley and turned the corner.

I waited there, crouched down and heart thumping against my ribs, tears freezing on my eyelashes and cheeks and then melting again when I blinked. My nose was running and I felt like I might throw up.

After a while my toes started to burn in the cold because I wasn't moving, wasn't keeping the blood flowing through them. Finally I stood up and peeked around the corner of the old wood-sided garage to the sleepy street. Nothing but snow falling and the blue glow of television sets in the living rooms of the houses on the silent street. A raven cackled from a power line and I jumped, and then laughed at myself a little. I pounded my hands together inside my mitts and stomped my feet. I was okay. I was fine. I was okay. Better to figure out now that the guy was an asshole than later. I ate some fresh snow off a fence post and swished it around in my mouth and spat it out. All I had to do was get home.

To this day the bus service in Whitehorse sucks. I pulled back the fur cuff of my parka and checked my watch, even though I already knew the answer. The last bus had headed downtown an hour ago, easy. Service up to Porter Creek where I lived had stopped much earlier than that. I pulled up the hood of my parka, wiped my nose on the back of my mitt, walked down to Lewes Boulevard, and stuck out my thumb. I knew there was a chance that Kevin would drive past. Just let him try to get me in his car, I thought. Let the fucker try. I dare him. I took stock of which of the houses close by still had their lights on.

A light blue Honda Civic hatchback pulled over right away. A girl I sort of knew from school was driving it. She had gone to one of the other junior high schools, but now went to the same high school as I did. She was in my chemistry class. She was nice enough. Let's say her name was Leslie, and that she played volleyball. Only one of these things is a lie.

She leaned over and pushed the passenger door open. "Get in. You must be freezing."

I got in. That song "Shout, shout, let it all out" was playing on the radio.

"You going downtown?" she asked me.

"Porter Creek, actually, but I will go as far as you can take me."

She met my eyes with hers. "You okay?"

I looked back at her. Tried to make my face a mask of nothing. I didn't know her. Didn't know who her friends were. Didn't know who she knew. The volleyball team. Not my people.

"I'm fine. I just missed the last bus and I need to get home."

"I can drive you all the way. I'm just going to get my brother from his hockey practice at Takini Arena. I'm early anyway. My dad was driving me nuts so I just left."

I sat back in the seat with a huge sigh. Pulled my mitts off and held my fingertips up to the heating vent in the dash.

She talked non-stop all through downtown and up the highway, sitting up too straight in the driver's seat like she was still nervous to be in control of a vehicle. Stopping fully at all stop signs, and not going too fast once we hit the highway. Windshield wipers thump-thumping, casting intermittent shadows across her wide face as the streetlights came and went above us.

She eased the car into our driveway. No one had shovelled it yet, that was my job.

"You can talk to me, you know." She put the car in park but didn't turn it off, and turned the radio down. "Centerfold" by the J. Geils Band. "I can keep my mouth shut," she said.

I don't know why I didn't trust my initial gut instinct and just keep my mouth shut. I can't even let myself think about how different the next three years of high school might have been for me if I had just kept my mouth shut that night in the volleyball player's car in my driveway.

"Kevin kind of … crossed a line with me tonight. Made me do something I didn't really want to do."

"Kevin your boyfriend Kevin? From the basketball team? Cute Kevin with the curly hair?" Her eyes were wide.

I regretted the words already, while they were still hanging in the air between us.

"Just forget about it," I said. "It wasn't a big deal. Thanks for the ride. I really appreciate it."

Her face shone white under the motion detector light that kept coming on and switching off above us. I had helped my dad install it a couple summers ago, passing tools up the ladder to him and listening to him explain about photovoltaic cells. She narrowed her eyes at me and leaned in.

"I wouldn't say anything if I was you. He's the assistant captain and will probably be the valedictorian this year. We're only grade tens."

I nodded. "Forget I said anything, okay? Thanks again."

She didn't smile, didn't say goodbye, just put the car in reverse and backed slowly into the street, looking both ways. Her face all serious and still.

I took a very hot bath and that is when the real tears came. Down my face and into the bathwater.

I told my mom the next morning that I didn't feel good, which was not a lie, and stayed in bed until everyone else had left the house for work and school. It was a Friday.

I didn't go out much over the weekend, which is why I didn't find out about the brand new couple until Monday morning in the cafeteria. Leslie and Kevin. Everyone was talking about it. How they got together at Brad's party on Saturday night. Everyone told me how good I was taking it. "You don't even seem that upset," Wendy who played oboe wrote me a little note in French class and passed it to me.

"Because I'm not," I wrote back.

I never told anyone what happened that night, not for years. Leslie and Kevin spent the rest of that school year making sure I was not invited to any of the cool parties, and things only got nominally better when he graduated and left town for university the following September.

The summer I turned nineteen, I ended up in the bar at the Klondike Inn on my birthday, drinking pitchers of draft beer and listening to a cover band do a pretty decent version of "Radar Love" by Golden Earring. I would have liked the band better had I not known that the lead singer had given a young woman I worked with at the Westmark Hotel waiting tables a nasty dose of chlamydia.

There were about fifteen of us loosely seated at a cluster of tables. At any given time a handful of us were up dancing or getting a drink. All of a sudden I found myself seated alone, and Kevin sat down at the table next to me. I had not seen him come in. He was wearing a pink short-sleeved shirt with the collar popped up. He was furrier, his eyebrows thicker, and he had too much stuff in his hair. He still wore the same aftershave.

He grabbed an empty glass and stared at the dregs. "I heard you're a dyke now. Is that true?"

I picked up the full pitcher of beer from the middle of the table and made like I was going to pour some for him. He held the glass up. Then I redirected, and emptied the entire pitcher right into the crotch of his jeans. He jumped up with a furrowed brow and his wet mouth open.

"Fucking bitch. What's wrong with you?"

"I heard you're a rapist now. I know that's true." I spun on the grass-stained heel of my work boot and left the bar.

Kevin went on to work for the government. I never told anyone what he had done. I didn't tell anyone until just recently. Sometimes Facebook suggests we should be friends. He is balding and still has the same thick, wet lips. I don't click on his profile. I don't want to find out that he has a pretty wife and teenage daughters now. I don't want to see him smiling at barbecues with guys I went to school with. I thought about blocking him but that would involve clicking on his profile, and sometimes I still entertain fantasies of sending him a well-worded and eloquent message threatening to write his wife and boss and tell them what he did that night in Riverdale in his parents' rec room. What he did that night, and what he did after, too. I don't believe that he turned himself around, that inside he was truly a good person who just made a mistake and that he has spent the rest of his life respecting women and working to make himself a better man. I don't believe any of those things.

It was the Jian Ghomeshi case that unlocked my mouth about it. I couldn't stand it anymore. All those asshats saying that there wasn't any proof. Guys I knew, guys I used to trust saying shit like that. That she was just doing it to get back at him for spurning her. That it was professional jealousy. That it was consensual. Why didn't they come forward sooner? they said. Like talking about this shit is easy. Like being called a slut in the comments is nothing. Like putting your private life and pain out there to be mocked and questioned and made into headlines doesn't cost you.

As if there is any possible thing to gain except for lifting the dirty truth off of your chest so you can finally breathe.

I'm saying I believe those women so I can believe myself. I'm saying I know what happened because I was there, too. I'm saying I understand their silence because I'm finally just writing about this thirty years later.

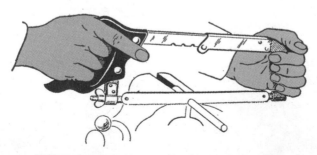

BOTH HANDS ARE USED IN HACKSAWING

# FRENCH KISSING

I got pretty serious about playing that saxophone. Played my scales in my upstairs bedroom until I bit a permanent dent inside my lower lip where it curled over my bottom teeth and pressed into my mouthpiece. I took home records and copped the saxophone solos off them, carefully transcribing the notes on music paper that my mom bought me special from the music rentals window at the back of Hougen's Department Store on Main Street.

Sometimes before my Mom quit drinking, she and her girl-friends would wake me up in the middle of the night, smelling like white wine or gin-and-tonics and laughing until they swore they were about to pee themselves. My mom would flip the light on in my bedroom and I would sit up, squinting and confused, trying to focus my eyes and figure out if it was morning already or still night time.

"Play 'Misty' for me," she would say, her words just a little bit slurred and her eyes wet. "Or the new song, with the sax bit, guilty feet have got no rhythm. Play us that one." So I would, I would spread my sheet music out on the blue and white shag carpet in my bedroom and play "Misty" for my mom and her friends, sleep-sweat sticking my pajama shirt to the skin between my shoulder blades and my hair all flat on one side until they got quiet and nodded and then went back downstairs and turned up Gordon Lightfoot or Abba and refilled their drinks.

At school we didn't have a trombone player for stage band, or enough of what our band teacher called "bottom end," so he asked me if I wanted to play the baritone saxophone as well. I loved the alto, but the first time I managed to gather up enough breath to blow a real note on that horn that was nearly as big as I was, I knew. I belonged in the bottom end. The band teacher would give me both trombone parts, the bari part and the alto part, for each song he assigned, and I would flip through them all and pick out the best bits from each and create my own hybrid score of awesome. I'd carry both horns home every night, my fingers cramping in the cold and my backpack full of books, sweating inside my parka even on the coldest days of winter as I huffed through the bare willow trees and silent lodgepole pines and frozen blue spruce, following the skidoo tracks up and down the sides of the little valley of bush that separated our house from the new junior high school on Hickory Street.

I don't remember anyone complaining about me practicing ever, not once, not even my sister, which amazes me now when I think about it. I played every night and no one ever told me to shut up or keep it down. This seems so unlikely that I just called my mom up in the Yukon to confirm my memories of it.

"How come you never ever told me to shut up, not once? The baritone saxophone? I played it once here in my apartment and my neighbour told me the next day in the elevator that it rattled the artwork on his walls. That thing is loud. I played it for hours every night. How did I not drive you crazy with it?"

She sounded distracted on the other end of the line. I glanced at the clock: 8:22 p.m. I had caught her in the middle of *Midsomer Murders.*

"It was never an issue for me. I liked it," she said. "You just kept getting better, I could hear you working little bits out and then doing them over and over. I was glad you had something that made you that happy. And your dad worked late almost every night back then."

By the middle of October of my last year in high school, everyone was talking about what to do next. Go to mechanic's school in Edmonton like Shaun White wanted to? Charlaina Ross was going to France because she had an uncle there or something. Claudette MacGowan was going to take computer science. Kim Rumley was going to be a social worker. Sandra James already had a good union job at NorthWestel, who needed university anyways?

I wanted to study music. There was a two-year university transfer program at a community college near where my cousin was living in North Vancouver. I wanted to study music but it seemed kind of like a silly dream, a dream a seventeen-year-old small-town girl might have until she got pregnant or married or both, or had to take a job as a clerk in a grocery store to pay the bills. It seemed like the plot of a music video or a gritty movie where eventually the main character has to come to their senses and face reality.

I went into the office in the back of our band room and waited for our band teacher Mr. Campbell to get back from his lunchtime meeting in the staff room.

"What's up, kiddo?" he smelled like coffee and Old Spice deodorant. His hair was always perfect, chocolate brown with just a few grey hairs slicked back from his temples. All of the girls at school thought he was handsome. Shadow of a beard. I thought he looked a little too much like a Lego man, with his exceptionally square jaw. I liked the way the veins bulged in his neck when he played the trumpet, though. I liked how he talked about how his wife was smarter than he was.

"I want to go to music school," I said. "I have straight As. Almost no one in my family has ever gone to university, and my mom wants me to go to law school. But I want to study music. My dad says the night shift at White Pass is full of mechanics that wanted to play guitar. So do you think I have what it takes to be a musician?"

He looked straight at me, stopped drumming on his desk with the eraser end of his pencil.

"I think that being a musician is like being any other kind of artist," he said. "All kinds of people are always going to tell you that it's a waste of time, to get a real job, that it will never pay, that you are not good enough. I want you to hear this, because it is important: my opinion is only one opinion. I am only one person. And if you are going to take the opinion of any one person that is not you and make a decision as important as what you want to do with your life based on what one person says, then I would say that you don't have what it takes to be an artist. But if you are going to do what I think you are going to do, and not listen to what anyone says and do what you feel most called to do, then I say go for it. Go to music school while you are young. Learn everything you can. Only one way to find out and that is by doing it."

So I did it. I moved into a two-bedroom basement suite in North Vancouver with my cousin who was dating a guy named Drew with an electronic monitor on his ankle because of "a little misunderstanding" he had about a few cars he was selling. Started music school. Class piano. Saxophone lessons. Choir. Ear training. Music history. I tried out for stage band and made it. Second alto. Someone was already playing the baritone saxophone. Her lips looked soft and her hair even softer. She wore black eyeliner and drove a teal blue 1967 Mustang. Her name was Ellen.

I drove an orange '74 Volkswagen van that I had to park facing down a hill so I could jumpstart it every other time I turned the key.

Ellen lived in a red brick and stone apartment building in the West End with two actors. One of them had a very famous brother, a Canadian kid who had struck it big with a sitcom in the States. The roommate with the famous brother wouldn't take his money so he bought her fancy gifts instead, like the leather-bound complete works of Shakespeare and a brand new camera and tripod. Ellen used to have horn sectional practice in her tiny living room on some Friday nights, six or seven of us crammed in there, the trombone players emptying their spit valves onto little bits of rag they put down on top of the worn out hardwood floor. We would play until the downstairs neighbours thumped on their ceiling with a broomstick, then pack up our horns and drink a beer or two and go home.

Except for the night of October 13, 1988. We wrapped up horn practice around ten o'clock. The night felt warm to me, especially for a Yukon kid still new to the city. I had parked my van around the corner, and when I climbed in and tried to start it, I couldn't get it to turn over. I crawled underneath it and whacked the starter with the back end of a crescent wrench like my uncle Rob had showed me to. Nothing. Not even a click. Parking was so tight in the West End that I had been forced to park on a little bit of an uphill slope, and the car in front of me had boxed me in. No way to push-start myself. I got out and walked back to the front door of Ellen's apartment building, buzzed number 306.

"Uh, it's me again. My van is broken down. I think I need to use your phone and call a tow truck or something."

Ellen had changed into sweatpants and put her hair up. Taken her makeup off. "Come on in." She stood on one foot and then the other in her doorway, waving me in with one hand. "My roommate has been dating another actor guy who works at a mechanic's shop. I think he's staying here tonight. You should just wait until they get back, maybe he can help you."

We sat at opposite ends of a rose-pink satin antique couch and drank beers. Talked about school, about music, about our band conductor, about the first alto guy who showed up late almost every practice but then blew the best solos so we nearly forgave him for the egg yolk stains on his one good concert shirt and his chronic tardiness.

I don't remember her suggesting that I spend the night there when her roommate and her mechanic boyfriend never did show up, but I am sure that is what must have happened, because I never would have asked. She was a jazz singer with a real band and gigs at the Railway Club and a funky apartment. She owned more than one pot for heating up soup in. I was eighteen and she was twenty-nine. She was way out of my cool zone and I knew it.

The curtains in her bedroom had the same pattern on them as the accent pillows on her bed. She lent me a way-too-big-for-me t-shirt to sleep in, which I changed into in the bathroom, folding my jeans and shirt and socks into a tidy pile and placing them right next to my boots just inside her bedroom door. She lit a candle on her desk with a match.

The pillow smelled like shampoo. Her feet were cold and mine were not. I don't remember thinking about kissing her, or even touching her, but my heart was thrumming in my throat, and I could hear the blood in my veins pumping past my eardrums. I was on my side and felt the heat of her behind me, an electric magnet feeling pulling at the little space between us. I did not move, I barely even breathed.

She slid a cool hand around my waist and let it rest on my belly. We stayed like that for a really long time, talking in the dark.

And then she moved her hand. I thought about stopping her, but didn't. And then she moved her hand again, pushed her hips into that curve where my ass became thighs.

I remember staring at myself in the foggy mirror of her bathroom the next morning.

"I kissed a girl. I kissed a girl," I whispered. When I opened the bathroom door, fully clothed and smelling like Ellen's deodorant and the communal Dr. Bronner's peppermint soap, her roommate Denise was standing there.

"Hey kiddo. Walter's making omelettes. Then he's going to see what's up with your van."

I was sure she could see it all over me, my queerness, my girl-kissing tendencies, but she breezed past me with a flip of her hair and turned on the shower.

No one said a word at breakfast, nobody asked why I had spent the night or looked at either of us sideways. Nothing.

I told no one. Who would I tell? My mom? No way. My classmates? My friends from high school? I didn't know any other gay people besides Ellen and me, and Ellen said she wasn't really gay, she just liked people, not their bodies. She just liked me, she said, no matter what bits I had or didn't have.

"If it's no big deal, how come we haven't told your roommates yet, or the guys in your band?" I asked her. She shrugged and said she would tell them when it was the right time.

So I carried her around in my secret inside pocket for a while, the smell of her perfume getting caught in the collar of my shirt, finding her long hairs in my clothes when I folded the laundry. Pretending not to watch her in band practice. Showing up at her gigs and sitting with her roommates and their friends from acting school and the thee-ah-tah.

"You got a boyfriend?" her piano player would slur in between sets and slide his chair closer to mine.

"Yeah," I would lie. "He works as a welder on an oil rig up in the Beaufort Sea."

"Sounds like a tough guy," he'd say, getting up to go get another beer.

"He is," I'd tell him, looking him straight in the eyes without smiling.

Later that semester I went into a barbershop, paid an old Italian guy named Mino ten bucks, and asked him to cut off all my hair. The piano player stopped asking me about my boyfriend after that. Stopped buying me beers, too.

Once I came out, I stayed out. I got a regrettable pink triangle tattoo on my shoulder and plastered Queer Nation stickers on my leather jacket and went to kiss-in protests at the old coffee shop on Commercial Drive. I wanted to fight homophobia everywhere, in everyone. I wanted to Act Up, to act out, to have sit-ins, and not stand for it anymore.

I wish now I had been kinder to my mother about it all.

Ellen moved into a big house in East Vancouver and started to date a guy who played trombone in her jazz quintet. I told her I couldn't spend too much time with her and all her straight friends anymore lest I be homogenized by their infectious heterosexuality. My politics didn't leave anyone, including me, a lot of room for nuance, or grey areas.

I wish I had been kinder to a lot of people about it all, come to think of it.

I met an old man today. Stanley used to be an electrician and he bought
that big old house thirty-seven years ago for sixty-eight thousand and now
it's worth a million maybe more but who cares what does that mean when
he's not selling? How is he going to pay the tax on that you tell me? He
asks me where did I get that lamp? What did I pay? He looked shocked.
Said he was just looking for a goddamn lamp to better read his paper by
now its winter but he went to Home Depot and they were all so expensive.

I told him that I was getting rid of the one that I was going to replace
with this one I had just bought. I said I could drop it by tomorrow.

He said 1803 William Street, just leave it around the side under the
awning next to the garbage if no one answers the door. Can't hear the
doorbell if I'm watching the home and garden channel, he said.

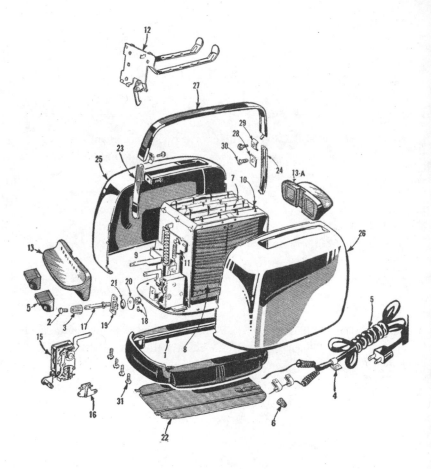

# WORK EQUALS FORCE TIMES DISTANCE OVER TIME

I worked as a landscaper for a few years when I first got to Vancouver. It was wet, dirty, hard work, but I loved it. I loved how hungry I was by the time dinner was ready after a long day outside, and how deep I slept. Loved the sight of a perfectly mowed lawn, a weedless flowerbed, a freshly trimmed hedge. Loved feeling my thighs grow hard and my biceps curl into apples from the labour. Permanent farmer tan and the smell of new topsoil. We worked in North and West Vancouver a lot, on huge properties that overlooked the ocean or had icy streams running through them. When you turned the hedger or weedwhipper or leaf blower or lawnmower off, it was quiet. Rich neighbourhood kind of quiet. No sirens, no traffic. Just squirrels and cedar trees waving in the wind and sometimes the sound of someone else's landscapers mowing or trimming something up the street.

It was the end of October, and work was getting scarcer and more difficult, and the mornings were cold. Most of the maintenance kind of landscaping was over until the spring, it was mostly just raking leaves and planting bulbs, building retaining walls or laying brick walkways. Hard on the back. Our boss took a contract to put in an underground sprinkler system in a giant McMansion up near 70th and Granville somewhere. The owner's son had gold-plated rims on his dark purple sports car, I remember that.

We were there for days, digging trenches for the irrigation

pipes in the hard-packed clay and big tree roots in the back yard. It never stopped raining once, not for a second.

We would sit in the truck on our breaks with the windows rolled up and steamy, the heater on full blast, holding our hands up against the vents to chase the ache and stiffness out of our fingers so we could go back to clutching the shovel or pick handle for another couple of hours. I would try to dry my boots out at night next to the heater but they would still be half wet in the mornings, and we would all be the same colour of mud from head to toe come five o'clock every night. The kind of work that makes you

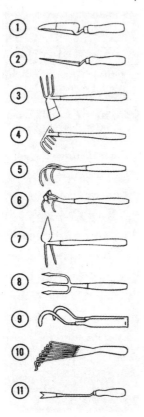

seriously reconsider your life choices about every ten minutes, all day, every day.

It was a Friday, and the rain was coming down sideways. I was digging a trench right alongside the house, and I had just ripped a hole right through my raincoat, my work shirt, and the skin of my upper arm on a rough piece of drainpipe. The side door of the house opened up and three workers came out wearing clean Carhartts and work boots, their leather tool pouches slung jauntily over their shoulders, pushing a shiny red tool chest on heavy casters. They loaded it into a clean white windowless van and drove away. A to Z Electric, the sign on the van read, with a yellow lightning bolt striking between the A and the Z. Those guys looked clean. They looked dry and warm and had nice tool belts.

I signed up for the Electricity and Industrial Electronics program at the British Columbia Institute of Technology on my next weekday off, and started school that following January.

There were two women and me, and 650 guys in the Electrical Trades building. One of the women dropped out after about three weeks, she was quiet and slight, a single mother with four kids. I don't remember her name now but I remember missing her after she was gone. I wanted her to graduate with honours and get a union job. I wanted her to be one of those stories. The ones they would put in the pamphlet. Take pictures of her wearing an orange reflective vest and a white hard hat and put it on a poster. I think she lasted nearly a month and just didn't come back one Monday morning.

The other woman was a tall, foul-mouthed waitress named Nikki with two K's and her dark roots showing. I liked her immediately, and we sat next to each other at the same table in class every day.

Nikki and I basically had the women's bathroom on the second floor of the Electrical Trades building all to ourselves, like it was our office. We would smoke cigarettes at lunch in there on rainy days, her sitting on one end of the counter top with her sensible shoes resting on the lip of the sink, me at the other end, my one shoulder propped against the paper towel dispenser, my grass-stained steel-toed work boots leaving dried up bits of tread-shaped mud on the countertop. Sometimes we would laugh in there until her mascara ran. She would run her pink lipstick-stained butts under the tap and then flick them into the silver trashcan, and check the corners of her mouth and scrunch her hair up in her fists and make a pouty face in the mirror before we went back to class.

The only other women in the building worked in the kitchen downstairs and used the bathroom on the ground floor. The women who worked in the kitchen smiled at Nikki and me when they passed us our chicken burgers with fries at lunch, asked us how school was going, like they were sort of proud of us but also didn't trust us. We weren't one of them anymore, and we had our own bathroom upstairs to prove it.

Nikki liked Bon Jovi and really tight jeans and she flicked her long hair like she learned how from a Guns 'N' Roses video and talked like she was from the prairies, which she was. I was the only lesbian she knew, she told me, except for maybe a woman who lived down the hall in her building, but she didn't know for sure, except she had the same haircut as me.

She might just be German, I said, making a joke, but Nikki nodded like she thought this might be a possibility.

I kept my mouth shut as much as I could in class and worked hard, doing a couple of hours of homework every night. Most of the guys in the class had been told all through school that they weren't university material, or they weren't related to anyone who had ever been university material. Lots of them spoke English as a second or third or fourth language, and most of them had saved up their tuition and living expenses working hard labour jobs. A lot of them really struggled with the math and algebra portion of electrical theory.

Both Nikki and I had sailed through math in high school, and a couple weeks into classes we found ourselves tutoring several of our male classmates through power factor calculations and word problems after school. They had names like Tyler and George and Mustafa, and they were farmers and pizza delivery guys and line cooks. Many were still working nights and weekends to pay the bills, nodding off in class in the first part of the morning until coffee break when they got some fresh air and a double-double into them.

I grew up around very capable men, and I also grew up sort of thinking that being raised male meant certain kinds of knowledge came with the territory. When we moved out of the classroom and into the shop for the more practical hands-on parts of school, I was surprised to find how many guys hadn't learned things I took for granted that men just somehow learned by osmosis. I couldn't believe that Edward, who sat right behind me and was smart and funny and bespectacled, didn't know how to cut a two-by-four on a right angle with a hand saw. In fact he didn't even know what a two-by-four was. Ritchie from Hope had spent a couple years in juvie already but somehow didn't know a Robertson screwdriver from a Phillips.

I found myself grateful to my dad and my uncles, and my aunts too, for everything they had taught me. All those hours in my dad's shop, in my uncle Rob's boat, tagging along while my dad and his brothers built our new house on Grove Street. I had already learned more from them than most of the guys in my class at school. I knew a little about how to weld, some basic mechanics, a little carpentry, some electronics from my Great Uncle Jack, and now some electrical stuff. It was easy to do well.

About ten weeks into school, the first round of marks were posted in the hallway on the second floor of the building, right outside the administration office. I was top of my class, and Nikki wasn't too far behind. I'm not sure if what happened next was a coincidence, or if it had to do with me having some of the highest grades in the class.

I noticed my locker first. Someone had written FUCK OFF DIKE on my locker in bold felt marker. I took my books out, found an empty locker at the opposite end of the hallway, and moved all my stuff into it. Same handwriting, same felt marker had written PUSSY EATERS on my and Nikki's table, so I just dragged it into the classroom across the hall and swapped it for a graffiti-free one. I felt bad about the table, though; since Nikki was a dedicated cock lover, I felt like the plural bit was sort of uncalled for.

I always arrived to school early, so all of this got done before most of my classmates got there. Nikki hadn't seen the table and I didn't tell her about it. When I first started electrical school, my grandmother Patricia had given me a little advice on working in a very male-dominated environment, as she had done for most of her life. "Pick your battles," she had told me. "Don't stand in front of the river. There will not be enough time in the day for you to take them all to task for every off-colour comment, for every slight against women, for every nonsensical thing they are about to say or do in your company. You are in a man's world and they will all feel obligated to remind you of this on a daily basis. Only tackle the important offenses, and always do it one on one, alone, just you and whichever asshole you can no longer tolerate. Never challenge him in front of his peers. That will get you nowhere at all. Take him aside, and whatever you do, don't cry. Save your tears for the car ride home. I always did."

So I said nothing to no one and went to class like it was any other day. Maybe that is why what happened next happened, because he didn't get a rise out of me the first go-round.

Our class had about thirty guys, plus Nikki and me. A couple of months in, we finally got to leave the classroom and spend some dedicated time in the shop, actually touching tools and wiring things. Our instructor, a small but terrifying old German guy named Dr. Wetzelmeyer, would draw a simple electrical blueprint on the board, like a light fixture switched from two different places, and a couple of electrical outlets, and then we would wire them up on our own little section of a plywood wall.

I really dug this part of electrical school. The circuits we were assigned to wire got slowly more complicated, and I never got tired of that moment when Dr. Wetzelmeyer would look over my work and nod his curt and moustached yes and I would get to plug my circuit in and watch the light bulb glow or the amber light blink. Electricity was both magical and logical at the same time. If you wired everything correctly in the right order, it worked. An invisible power somehow coursed through the wires and made stuff happen. Lights went on and switches worked and fans hummed and heating elements glowed.

I was proud of my toolbox, and kept everything inside it neat and orderly. I had saved up and invested in a set of top-of-the-line Klein screwdrivers, and I loved the heavy, balanced rubber grips on them. Loved picking them up and feeling their solid heft in my palm. My circuits were all right angles, wires tacked equal distances apart from each other, my screws flush and straight and tight. I pretty much took everything I had learned from my father in his shop and my uncles on different jobsites and applied it to my projects, and nearly every day our instructor pointed out my work to the rest of the class as an example of the kind of attention to detail that would make me into a fine tradesman. It made me proud enough that I didn't need to mention the man part. I was proving to the guys in my class that I was every bit as much of an electrician as they were, and that was what mattered to me. I liked the order and math and measurement of it all. I liked that it required skill and could be dangerous if you made a mistake or didn't know what you were doing. It made a

kind of easy and natural sense to me, and every day that passed
in the shop I grew more and more sure that I was really going to
love this job once I got out of school, and that I was going to be
good at it.

One day I came back from lunch a little earlier than the rest of
my class. It was a Friday and I was nearly finished wiring a particularly challenging circuit and really wanted to complete it before the
weekend. I flipped the light switch in the doorway to the back room
where all the plywood walls were mounted. The fluorescent lights
flickered and then hummed to life. The room smelled like plywood
and Pine-Sol and dust burning on the baseboard heaters and wet
rain jackets left slung over the backs of chairs clustered around the
desks in one corner of the workroom.

I turned on the radio that sat in the weak middle-of-March
sun on a windowsill and spun the dial from top forty to CBC and
turned it up.

I reached into my spotless toolbox for a Robertson No. 3 screwdriver and felt something wet and almost warm. At first I thought
the roof was leaking, but when I looked up I couldn't see any evidence of this. I picked up my toolbox and carried it over to the
industrial sink in the corner of the workroom and held my tools
inside with one hand and tipped it upside down to empty the water
out of it. Except it wasn't water. It was piss. I could smell it. One
of the dudes in the building had pissed into my toolbox. I dumped
everything into the sink and started wiping it all down with paper
towels. My brand new multi-meter that my mom had given me for
Christmas. I had to peel off its rubber case to clean it properly,
gagging a little bit and trying to blink through the tears I could not
keep from welling up in my eyes. I looked at the clock on the wall.
I had eleven more minutes to get this cleaned up and get myself

together before everyone else started trailing in after the lunch break. I was certainly not going to give whoever had done this the satisfaction of seeing me scrubbing their piss from the inside of my beloved toolbox, and I for sure wasn't about to let any of them see me cry about it.

I was whistling quietly and listening to the CBC and wiring away on my project wall by the time the first of my classmates came in. Pretending like nothing was wrong. My toolbox was dry and spotless and neat, just like it always was. I studied all of their faces as they strolled in through the door, trying not to look like I was checking them out. It couldn't be Tyler or George or Mustafa or Edward, I told myself. None of those guys would do something so disgusting to anyone, let alone one of their classmates. It might not have even been a guy in my class; it could have been any one of the 650 dudes in the Electrical Trades building. But how would they know which toolbox was mine, I wondered? It had to be one of my classmates, unless the school had a random toolbox pisser on their hands. What were the odds that it was not a targeted thing? Was I being paranoid or realistic?

Everyone returned from lunch. No one else had a toolbox full of someone else's urine. No one looked guilty. I didn't tell Nikki, because I knew she would stomp about and swear and make a scene, and I didn't want to deal with a scene. Even though I loved her scenes, and they were always justified and awe-inspiring to behold, I just couldn't deal that day. Besides, I had already cleaned up all the evidence.

But I found myself watching my classmates carefully after that day. Watching their eyes to see if they would meet mine. Watching their body language. Watching my back.

I knew it wasn't Tyler or George or Mustafa or Edward. They

were my friends. Tyler stopped by his grandmother's house every Thursday to take the garbage cans out to the curb and rake leaves and swap her snow tires off her car and listen to her tell the same stories over and over again, and George was raised in Poland and brought both Nikki and me flowers on International Women's Day because it was a national holiday in his country. Mustafa and Edward were both gentle and soft-spoken. I just couldn't see it being any of them. Nikki and I were spending an hour after school at least once a week helping them with their math, or explaining things in slower English than our instructors used in class. After a week or so of wondering, I tried to put it all out of my mind.

There was a really quiet giant of a man who sat across the aisle from me in class. His name was Bruce, or maybe Bill. Something with a B. Brian? I think it was Bruce. He barely spoke, never asked questions, and got a solid B minus on all of his tests. I didn't take much notice of him other than to note that he often smelled like wood smoke when he first sat down in the mornings, before he took his GWG jean jacket off.

One day just as we were wrapping up at the end of class, he stood awkwardly in front of my desk, his backpack slung over one shoulder, swallowing and blinking repeatedly as I packed up my textbooks and notes.

"Have you, uh, got a minute to spare for me?" He rested his considerable bulk on one foot, and then the other. "You, know, uh, privately?"

"Sure, thing Bruce." I smiled at him. "Math question?"

He shook his head slowly. "My name is Barry. It's not a math thing. It's personal."

"I'm sorry. Barry. Right."

We waited while everyone else cleared out of the room. I motioned for him to sit down next to me. He stayed standing. Seemed to re-consider. Turned a chair around and straddled it, resting his furry forearms on the chair back. Squeaked the chair forward and leaned over my desk and spoke quietly.

"I need marriage advice," he confessed.

"But I'm not married," I told him.

"Yeah, well, but you know women, right? I mean, more than I would, you know? Since you date them plus you are one, I just figured, I don't know, I hope I'm not offending you, really, maybe this is all a stupid idea, I just thought ..." He squirmed in his chair, squinting one eye nearly shut at me.

"I'm not offended." I smiled at him.

He let out a long breath.

"Just try me. If I can help, I will." I smiled again, raised my eyebrows a little.

"It's my wife and I," he leaned even farther forward. "We, uh, haven't been ... intimate much for the last while. The last year or so. Maybe closer to two years, you know? We used to be all over each other. Even after our son was born, and I hear from other couples that sometimes when a kid comes along things ... slow down in that department, you know? But that never happened with us."

I nodded to him to keep on talking. He did.

"But a couple of years ago she went back to school to get her Master's, plus she works nearly full time, and that's I think when we started to, well, grow apart a little? So, I uh, thought maybe you might have some ... you know, insight? Advice? I dunno. What do women want? Any ideas?"

Barry was blushing hard, a red stain oozing out of his chest hair and up his neck, throbbing in his big round ears. He looked so cute, I felt like hugging him.

"I feel like hugging you right now," I said.

He sat back a little, eyes wide. Put the palms of both hands flat on the desk between us.

"I won't," I reassured him. "But you are incredibly sweet right now."

His cheeks glowed crimson. He stared at his square fingernails like they were suddenly a complete mystery to him.

"She's tired," I told him. "I don't claim to know what women want, or what anyone really wants, for that matter, but I bet you any money she is tired as shit all the time right now. I bet I know what might help."

He sat up straight, his eyes met mine and stayed there.

"When does she get home from school tomorrow night?"

"Uh, tomorrow's what, Thursday? Around 7:30 on Thursdays."

"You get home around four or so? Plenty of time. Okay. Here's what you're going to do."

He took his pen out of his pocket and started to write.

"First off, send the kid to grandpa and grandma's house for the night if you can. Second, clean the house. I mean clean the house. Vacuum, mop the kitchen floor, and change the sheets on the bed. Scrub the bathtub and clean the toilets. Put a new toilet paper roll actually on the holder thingy. Get a scented candle. Not a cheap one. I will give you the address of a place on the Drive. Get her some bubble bath while you're at it, too. Do at least two loads of laundry. Do the dishes and, write this down, buddy. Put them away. In the cupboards." I checked his list. He had very tidy handwriting. I took this as a sign of his great potential to succeed with this mission. I continued.

"Get some flowers. You don't have to spend a fortune. Just a little bunch. And bust out the good napkins. Set the table. Then all you need is a chicken to roast and some yams and potatoes and broccoli, and a decent bottle of wine. I'll write the recipe down to make home-made gravy. It's easy. You can do this. Put the chicken in the oven around an hour before she is supposed to get home. Open the bottle of wine. Don't pour any until she gets home and takes her shoes off and pees and finds out you cleaned the tub and scrubbed the toilets. And be wearing her apron, if she has one, over your own clothes. No t-shirt. Wear a button-down. Seriously. No t-shirt. Make sure your socks match and wear your best underwear, because if all goes well she is going to be in them right after you finish dinner."

He tilted his head. "Wear her apron?"

"Trust me on this. Wear her apron. At least until you are about to serve dinner. Eat dinner, drink some wine, and then pour her a bath. In the clean tub. With the candle and the bubble bath. After she's done her bath go down on her for at least twice as long as you ever have before. Start slow. Don't walk right up to the front door and ring the doorbell right away, if you know what I mean. Commit yourself. Don't be cheap with the head. And shave first. Like, shave at five o'clock. Let me know on Tuesday how it all goes. Have a great long weekend. Happy Easter, dude."

Barry spent a few minutes writing it all down like a champ, asked for clarification on the finer points of both gravy-making and cun-nilingus, and then slipped his notebook back into his backpack and headed for the door.

I ended up in the lane next to his truck while I was driving home. He in his big truck and me in my little truck. He didn't see me, I don't think, his eyes were fixed straight ahead on the road in front of him, he took the ramp east onto the freeway, I went west. He was bobbing his head to the stereo. His hair was a little too long. I should have told him to hit the barber, I thought. His window was rolled down just a couple of inches. I caught a little bit of the song before he accelerated and disappeared into the traffic.

He was listening to k.d. lang. Her early stuff. I was starting to really like Barry.

I ended up going to Seattle for an S&M party, had a half-drunk threesome with a cute couple who both worked for Microsoft, and kind of forgot all about Barry and his marital woes until Tuesday morning when he sauntered into our classroom. He grinned with his whole face and opened both of his arms wide when he saw me and gave me the first and last hug I ever witnessed him engage in, right there under the fluorescent lights next to the desk I shared with Nikki.

Nikki shot me a suspicious look. I sat back down, shrugged, and whispered sideways that I'd helped him with a little bit of homework. She didn't ask any questions, and neither did I.

Barry smiled shyly at our shared secret for several months after that, and his wife hugged me at our class barbecue in June, and winked at me whenever she caught my eye all that night.

We graduated the following October. I ran into Tyler once a couple of years ago, at Costco, both of us waiting for the free chicken and rice samples to come out of the convection oven set up on a table in the frozen foods aisle. We got to gossiping about folks from school, and how had twenty years gone by anyway? Tyler told me he had heard through the grapevine a couple of years ago that Barry had died of some kind of cancer, of the pancreas maybe, leaving his wife and three kids behind.

Barry only had the one son, all those years ago when I instructed him to don his wife's apron and roast her a chicken.

I guess our plan must have worked.

I am talking to two of the construction workers who are almost finished building the new condo kitty-corner to mine. I ask them if the new apartments are nice. They are holding their coffees, looking up, shaking their heads. They're nice enough, they tell me, but small, and rents start at $1,350 a month for a studio, one guy says. "I can never afford the rents on the places we work on, much less the down payment, and I build them, fifty hours a week."

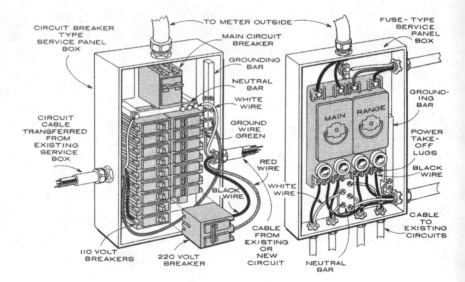

CIRCUIT BREAKER TYPE SERVICE PANEL BOX

TO METER OUTSIDE

MAIN CIRCUIT BREAKER

GROUNDING BAR

NEUTRAL BAR

WHITE WIRE

GROUND WIRE GREEN

RED WIRE

WHITE WIRE

BLACK WIRE

CIRCUIT CABLE TRANSFERRED FROM EXISTING SERVICE BOX

110 VOLT BREAKERS

220 VOLT BREAKER

CABLE FROM EXISTING OR NEW CIRCUIT

FUSE-TYPE SERVICE PANEL BOX

GROUNDING BAR

POWER TAKE-OFF LUGS

BLACK WIRE

CABLE TO EXISTING CIRCUITS

NEUTRAL BAR

MAIN

RANGE

# JOURNEY, MAN

I liked the journeyman electrician I was training under. James was a decent guy, the father of a three-year-old daughter, and from what I could tell, a good man. Sweet to his wife. We were working for a pretty big company, but for the most part, most days, it was just him and me. He never not once made cracks about having a female apprentice. He knew I had been top of my class, and that meant something to him. He had studied a bit of political science before he went into the trades. He read books. Played drums in a band. He wasn't a redneck, which was probably why the big boss had put us together.

We were working out in Surrey on a big condominium complex, installing the fixtures and plugs and switches in mostly finished suites. It was fairly easy, clean, and dry work. A bigger crew had wired the building earlier on in the heavy construction phase, and now it was just James and me, finishing up. Labelling electrical panels, testing everything, making it pretty, like he always said.

I was down in the electrical room in the underground parking lot of the four-storey condo building. James was upstairs in one of the residential units. It was a Friday. I was doing an inventory of our supplies, and cleaning up to leave the jobsite for the long weekend.

I heard James come over the walkie-talkie, which was already docked in the charger.

"Hey, it's 4:35 already. Where the hell are you? Let's get out of here."

I had lost track of the time. Quitting time was five minutes ago. I slung my tool pouch over my shoulder and locked the door behind me.

Nothing lonelier than a construction site five minutes after quitting time on a Friday.

The fluorescent lights hummed in the underground parking. I liked the wet smell of basement and concrete. James would be waiting in his brand new Ford F150 on the side street outside of the gate that led to the parking garage. We didn't have fobs to open the gate and had to park on the street all day while we were working. Part of every one of my workdays involved repeated trips to plug the parking meter on James' truck and moving it every few hours to avoid getting a ticket. This was a common pastime of apprentices from every crew on the site. It was a pain in the ass that James complained about at least twice a day.

I glanced at my watch. 4:41. We were going to get stuck in the middle of rush hour on the freeway heading back into the city and I was going to hear about it.

I had just rounded the corner from the second floor onto the first floor of the garage when I saw them. Six or seven dudes. The stucco guys, maybe? Or roofers? I had seen them coming and going here and there a couple of times over the last few weeks of working on this site, but I had never spoken directly to any of them. Up close I could see the white plaster dust on their work pants and steel-toed boots. Drywall guys, I thought. They stopped in a semi-circle in front of me.

I wasn't paying close enough attention at first to be scared right away.

I went to walk in between the skinny one and the really tall one, and the tall one sidestepped and closed the space between him and the skinny guy. They both looked at me. Gave each other sideways eyes. Looked back at me. This wasn't friendly. This was something else, I could smell it.

My heartbeat picked up and I snapped to attention. Counted six of them. Reached into my tool pouch. Rested my hand on a giant flathead screwdriver, about fourteen inches long. Dull but big. Every electrician has one in their pouch. It's called your beater screwdriver, and it is literally meant for beating on things. Knocking out pre-punched holes in panels and junction boxes, hammering lock-nuts tight on box connectors, prying open cans of paint or glue or lubricant, chipping wood away from the inside of holes you drilled, shit like that. Part chisel, part hammer, part screwdriver. My right hand rested on the fat black and red handle of my beater and counted. Six of them. There were six of them.

The tall guy stared at me, then let his eyes travel up and down my frame. The skinny guy looked at the concrete floor. All six of them shuffled closer together, closer to me.

I made a move to the left, and a dark-eyed guy with a filthy white t-shirt stepped in front of me. I stopped. Stepped back. Watched dirty t-shirt guy look over at the tall one, who nodded in approval. The tall guy seemed like he was in charge, so I locked eyes with him.

"You guys want to fuck around? Is that what this is?" I pulled the big screwdriver out of my pouch and held it up in front of me. Poked it into the space between me and the tall one.

"Well, there are six of you and one of me, but I will not make this easy for any of you. Someone is going to get this stuck in between their ribs. So who's first? You want to go first, Mr. Big?"

They all looked at the tall guy. He spat on the concrete between us. Sneered at me from under his moustache.

"What? What is your problem? There you go. Go home with your boyfriend," he said, stepping aside and holding out his right hand, arm outstretched like he was welcoming me through his front door.

I stepped between him and the skinny guy and managed not to break into a full-on run until they had rounded the corner onto the second floor of the underground.

Fucking drywall guys, I thought. What were they even doing down here? Concrete walls down here.

James had the classic rock channel cranked up when I climbed up into his truck.

"Took you long enough. I was about to come looking for you. Thought maybe you got lost."

I got in. Put my seatbelt on. Stared into the traffic.

"You're uncharacteristically quiet," he said about ten minutes later, resting his hand on the gearshift and sliding his eyes sideways to look at me. "Put the goddamn CBC on again if you want to."

I shook my head. My heart had slowed down by this time, but I felt the bile in my stomach threatening to boil up into my chest and throat.

"Seriously. What's up? You look pale. Did you see a ghost in the underground parking?"

We were stalled in traffic waiting to get onto the bridge when I finally told him what had happened. He cursed. He slammed his palms against the steering wheel. He swore he was going to call the site supervisor as soon as he got home and report the whole crew of drywall guys.

"For what, exactly?" I asked him calmly, staring straight ahead. "For standing in front of me in the parking lot?"

"You and I know full well that is not what they were doing." James was shaking his head. He reached over and snapped the radio off.

"Of course. But I can't prove anything. The word of six of

them against one of me. I'm one of two female tradespeople on the whole fucking site. Remember what a hassle it was to even get a second outhouse?"

The outhouse had been a weeks' long hassle, and Casey, the female plumber's apprentice, had nearly quit her job over it. The one outhouse on site was a disgusting mess. It was shared by about sixty guys, and it was a nasty bit of work. I had been walking about four blocks away to use the public bathrooms at the Burger King in the strip mall on the corner, but Casey took a stand. She went to the first aid guy and said it was a matter of health and safety for her and me, and that we wanted a women's biffy. It had been dropped off during the night finally, and was the object of much grumbling and glaring. Some of the guys complained that their biffy was filthy and started using ours. Someone had sharpied a giant cock and balls on the wall inside of it, and a couple of days after Casey and the rest of the plumbers had finished up and moved on to another site, I gave up and started going back to use the one at Burger King again. Some wise-ass had taped up signs on both outhouse doors, one that said "Clean," and another that said "Landscapers."

And that was the end of that.

"You can't go to the site supervisor and tell them the drywall guys stood in a circle around me in the parking lot. Nothing happened."

"This time," James said.

I turned the radio back on.

Sunday afternoon, James called me to tell me that he had just heard from the boss and we were not going back to Surrey after the long weekend. We were going to get laid off for a couple of weeks and then start a brand new job in New Westminster mid-month.

"Take a break," James said. "Put your feet up for a couple of days. I think I'm going to go fishing maybe."

"Did you tell Richard about those fucking drywall guys? Is that what happened?"

James promised me that he hadn't said a word, that it was just a slow time and that the boss was sending his knuckle-dragger of a nephew to finish up in Surrey.

I didn't know if I believed him or not, but I didn't care.

Two days later I got a call from a friend who was working on a movie set.

"Come check it out," she said. "The film business is full of freaks and weirdos. Good money. We need someone who can wire up props with flashing lights and shit. You're perfect for it."

She said she would pick me up at seven a.m. on Monday morning if I was into it.

"Call time is eight a.m., unless it gets pushed," she explained.

"What's a call time? What does that mean, pushed? So much lingo," I said.

"I'll explain everything in the van on the way to set. You're going to love it." She laughed. "It's a whole different world. Kind of like the army, except it's all make-believe. And the guns are fake."

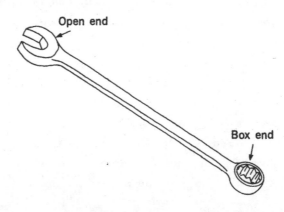

Elderly lady in public bathroom #1: "Excuse me, sir, you are in the ladies' room."

Lady #2: "Leave her alone, Roberta. She obviously needs to pee, to risk the likes of you. You're embarrassing us all."

# YOU CAN'T HANDLE THE TRUTH

In 2001 I was working on a film set, doing props for a television series. It was about journalists and terrorism and world events; it was actually a pretty decent show, and might have done okay if those airplanes hadn't flown into the two towers that September. Many of the show's plot lines corresponded too well with the actual current events rolling out on our televisions, and the series was shelved.

But that spring, before the planes crashed, before 9-11, we were shooting season one in Vancouver and the women who worked in the hair, makeup, and wardrobe departments decided that they were going to throw a party. The word went out: Saturday night at the head of the wardrobe department's big old house in North Vancouver. It was going to be epic, and it was ladies only, and I was invited.

The grips and lamp operators and camera guys all caught wind of this ladies only party and started giving me a hard time about it. "How come you're allowed to go?" The crane operator seemed particularly perturbed about it all. "The invite says Ladies Only. Right here." He stabbed the photocopied party invite with a giant sausage-shaped finger. "How is that even fair? You're more like one of us than them."

"Years of homophobia. Never being able to use a public fucking washroom. This is my pay-off. The ladies have spoken. I'm invited and you are not."

"It's ladies only. How come you get to go? I'm more of a lady than you are," said one of the gay set decorators.

I shrugged. "What do you care? There will be no action for you there anyway."

But by the time Saturday night rolled around, I was pretty tired, and I had just spent seventy hours that week with the whole crew, and I almost didn't go. I was curled up watching a movie at about eight p.m. that night when my cell phone rang. I ignored it, but it rang again. I picked it up on the fifth ring.

It was Sarah, a kind of bi-curious locations scout. "Ivan! Tell me you're on your way to this party right now. And tell me you are stopping to pick us up three more bottles of tequila gold and some white wine."

She sounded pretty drunk already. I got up, showered, and put some pants on.

I could hear the music thumping as soon as I rounded the corner and parked my shitty old Taurus behind the row of new mostly black cars and SUVs. All the lights in the house were on and a wall of party noise blasted me as soon as I walked through the front door. It smelled like beer and perfume and something almost burning in the oven.

Nearly every woman from the crew was there: the production assistants were smoking on the back deck, the wardrobe and makeup departments were playing a rambunctious game of Twister in the sunken living room, the female actors were gathered around a nearly scorched batch of breaded zucchini fingers someone had just taken out of the oven. The counters were already full of empty beer and wine bottles.

I held up the brown paper bag of booze I had procured on the way over and it was snatched out of my hand, and one of the hairdressers immediately began pouring tequila into shooter glasses arranged on a tray on the kitchen table. The white wine went directly into the freezer to chill.

One of the actors was named Jamie, and she was gorgeous in

that airbrushed kind of Hollywood way that always left me feeling underdressed and unfinished. The only interactions I ever really had with her were taking her prop watch on and off at the beginning and end of each shooting day, and occasionally when she needed something for her character or a scene. At work she always spoke to me in her private school British accent like I was the hired help, which technically I was. Not all of the talent, as we called the actors, treated the crew like we were less than, but Jamie certainly did. I had never liked her, and I was pretty sure she didn't even know my name.

But that night she was wearing jeans and a plain t-shirt, hardly any makeup, and was merrily forcing tequila shots on everyone, punctuated by her throwing one back herself every five minutes or so. She was cracking jokes and even let out a fart when she leaned over the arm of the couch to pass a shot glass to the third assistant director. I had never seen drunk and farting Jamie before, and I liked her a lot better than I did her on-set, at-work persona.

Lisa was there too, one of my favourite cast members. She had a couple of kids and lived in L.A. with her ex-husband and her new boyfriend. She told me one time she had learned to model her alternative family from all her queer friends, and that her kids had three loving parents and that was better than most kids could say. She was hilarious and real and we had hit it off the first minute of the first day of being on set together. She threw both of her arms around me and left a lipstick mark on my cheek. I had never seen her drunk before either. She smelled like hairspray and looked shorter without her character's signature high heels on.

I had never seen most of the women I worked with drunk. I had seen them wet, exhausted, hung over, on the first day of their periods. I had seen them at three o'clock in the morning and at midnight. I had seen them pumping their breast milk into a bag in the makeup trailer at lunchtime. I had seen them in rain gear and shorts and before coffee in the morning, but I had never seen them drunk.

At some point a Polaroid camera came out, and then several other cameras. This was back when cameras had film and cell phones weren't smart. The three bottles of tequila I had brought when I arrived disappeared, and someone phoned their husband and sent him on another liquor run. He wasn't even allowed through the front door with it; his wife the set decorator kissed him on the front porch, took the bag of booze, and shut the door behind her and locked it. She turned around, held up the brown paper bag, and everybody cheered.

I had been to a lot of queer parties where it was all women, but I had never been to a party full of only straight women before. They were ramping it up pretty good, drinking hard and telling disgusting jokes and laughing until they snorted and shot wine out of their noses. It was like being at a party with a bunch of kids with no adults around, but it was a party where there were no men, no husbands, no kids, and so, maybe for them, in some way, no one to impress or behave for. There was a kind of abandon in the room, a kind of unhinged freedom. These women could drink and cut loose without being watched by the guys at work, without being judged. Without worrying about getting caught in a corner somewhere with a handsy teamster or beer-brave grip. All of their defenses came down like a curtain. Drinks were getting kicked over and dishes were being broken. The Twister game was getting pretty racy and I remember wondering if bachelorette parties got this out of control this fast.

That's right about when the chocolate mousse cake appeared and things took a turn.

I think it was Jamie who first suggested we play Truth or Dare. This quickly turned into a round of Who At Work Would You Fuck If No One Would Ever Know, punctuated by long gulps of wine or a shot of tequila. I was taking it pretty easy on the booze because I had to drive back home over the bridge, but I seemed to be the exception.

"I would totally fuck Nathan," one of the caterers confessed.

Jamie gasped. "Nathan the cameraman? He's completely knock-kneed!" This sounded hilarious in her private school syllables, and then she cracked the whole room up by stumbling across the room with her knees pressed together like she was holding a quarter between them.

Then Jamie got quiet. "I know. We should do body shots."

"What's a body shot?" I asked, and the whole room exploded in another round of laughter, like there was no way I could possibly not know what a body shot was. I insisted I did not.

Jamie cleared her throat. "It's when, for instance, I would drink this delicious shot of tequila, and then lick salt and lime juice off of Lisa's lovely breasts."

She demonstrated for the room, to a loud round of cheering. Lisa responded by swiping a fingerful of chocolate mousse and wiping it on Jamie's cheek and licking it off. More whooping.

And so forth. The next thing I knew, a room full of drunk straight women were smearing chocolate mousse everywhere and licking it off each other, and someone was taking pictures of everything.

I'm not making this up.

I quickly realized that as the only out queer person in the room (as far as I knew), it just felt best for me if I remained a bystander. A straight married woman licking chocolate mousse off of her equally heterosexual coworker in a moment of tequila-induced abandon is one thing. A straight woman licking anything off of the only butch in the room, or vice versa, well, to me, that felt like something else. I felt like that might make Monday morning uncomfortable for someone, so I just watched.

And that is a true story.

Everyone was still going at it pretty serious when I left around midnight, quite sober, and drove home. I got an incoherent pocket call from Sarah the locations scout at about 3:30 in the morning. I could hear her giving directions to a cab driver and then it sounded like she was making out with an unknown female subject in the back seat of the taxi. I hung up the phone and went back to sleep.

Monday morning was fun, it was like all of us who had been there had our own giant, private, no boys allowed club-house secret. Lisa was already in the line-up for breakfast outside the catering truck when I got there. She grabbed me by the elbow and dragged me to one side, stage whispering.

"Everything that happened is classified. We're not telling any of the guys anything about the party. It's driving them nuts. Mum's da word. Pass it on. Got it?"

I nodded and she let my arm go.

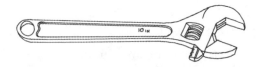

Several women who had been at the party were gathered in a circle on set just before call time. Much smirking and winking at each other ensued and knowing smiles were exchanged. The first assistant director was perusing her call sheet and the grips were setting up track for the camera dolly, and I was unfolding the director's chairs and arranging them around the monitor when Nathan, the cameraman, lumbered past us all, and nodded good morning to everyone. "Ladies," he fake-saluted to us all. He was so knock-kneed that his legs looked like a bony X as he strolled past and headed for the coffee and donuts table. We could barely wait until he was out of earshot to explode with raucous laughter.

By the time the coffee truck showed up at about ten o'clock in the morning, the rumours were flying fast. It wasn't because any of us were talking. It was because none of us were talking.

Grips, lamp operators, caterers, and male actors all tried to pry the details out of me.

"Ivan Coyote. On set props department. 604 ..." I kept repeating my name, department, and cell phone number like I was a captured soldier in enemy territory.

Then it all exploded. Lisa had left an envelope full of Polaroid shots from the party in the pocket of her cast chair and one of the set decorators snuck a peek at them before she snatched them out of his hands, but he started talking. All he had to do was mention Jamie and chocolate mousse and a body shot of tequila and the rumours replicated like a virus.

At one point late in the morning, I had to run up to the production office to pick up some beer can labels with a fake brand name on them that the art department had printed up for us, and one of the producers grabbed me by the sleeve and hauled me into his office, shutting the door behind us.

This guy was a Hollywood dude. He had produced some pretty decent television series in the past, and everyone was a little scared of him. He was demanding and didn't like shooting in Canada. He missed Los Angeles and told the entire crew all about it at every possible opportunity. He had also never spoken directly to me in six months of fourteen-hour days.

"Ivan. You are just the person I was looking for."

I didn't even know he knew my name. Suddenly he was looking for me? This couldn't be good, I thought.

"Tell me about this party on Saturday night. I heard it got pretty off the hook."

I turned my walkie-talkie down. Stood on one foot, then the other. "I ... uh, can't. I took an oath. I'm sworn to secrecy."

"Come on. Just between you and me. I won't tell anyone. Did Lisa really lick chocolate icing off Jamie's ... off Jamie?" He waggled his eyebrows at me, like we were old pals, like we chatted like this all the time.

I think his name was Kevin. Maybe it was Keith? I could Google it now, but I won't.

"Listen, man," I said. "That party was ladies only and I barely made the criteria as it was. I can't reveal anything at all. If I tell you anything, I won't be allowed to go to the next ladies only party, and I very much want to stay on that invite list."

"That good, huh?" He let out a low whistle and shook his head slowly.

"No comment." I nodded solemnly. He narrowed his eyes at me. "Sir," I added, and left his office door open when I exited.

By the time lunch rolled around, which happens six hours after morning call time in the film industry, the boys were whipped up into a full on fury of curiosity. The rain pounded on the roof of the lunch tent, and the propane heaters made the air inside warm and eggy.

We remained tight-lipped. The boys for some reason thought I was the most likely candidate to talk, but I remained steadfast in my silence. Saturday night, that party, it had been for us, not them, and we were keeping it.

Finally, the gaffer snorted out loud and threw his napkin onto his half-eaten plate of pasta, and fished around in his jacket pocket for his smokes. He stood up.

"They're just yanking our chains, boys. Nothing happened at that party. They're not telling us what happened because there is nothing to tell." He turned on his heel and stalked out of the lunch tent and into the rain to smoke.

Lisa licked her lips and smiled slow. She raised one perfectly shaped eyebrow into a question mark.

"That's right, Richard," she called after him. "We simply drank white wine and exchanged recipes and gossiped and supported each other as women."

All of us who were at the party cracked up. The boys crossed their arms.

Lisa pointed a manicured finger at the open flap of the door that Richard had just disappeared through and raised her voice, and did her best Jack Nicholson voice.

"You can't handle the truth!" she boomed.

Marguerite, one of my favourite hairdressers, stood up and made a beeline for the door, announcing that she was about to pee herself. She walked out holding her knees together, which all the boys thought was her not trying to pee her pants.

Everyone who had been at the party, of course, knew she was doing her best Nathan the cameraman impression, and we really lost it. Lisa laughed until she cried and her mascara ran and she had to head back to the makeup truck to get herself fixed up before we started shooting again.

I wasn't used to feeling like one of the girls, but I did that day, and I had to admit, it felt pretty good.

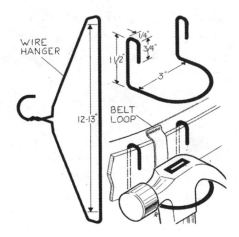

Me to a guy carrying a baby in a Snugli next to me in the grocery store line-up: "If you had a half-chewed piece of cracker stuck to the side of your head, would you want someone to tell you?"

Guy with baby says, with resignation: "Probably not."

"Well then," I say, "forget I said anything."

Linda Gould was a friend of my mom's. Linda was from somewhere not here, somewhere not the Yukon, she had family down south and she had raven black hair. One time I asked my mom why Linda's name was Linda Gould but her husband was still called Don Dixon. My mom told me that some women chose not to take their husband's last name when they got married. It was 1974 and this impressed me for reasons I did not fully comprehend just yet.

Linda and Don lived in a rented house next to the clay cliffs downtown, and had one wall in their living room covered in that mural type of wallpaper, depicting a picture of a forest of giant pine trees. Linda wouldn't let Don paint over that wallpaper or tear it down; she said it reminded her of California.

I was a Yukon kid and had never seen a real tree that big in my life, I could only imagine them.

Linda played hockey, and she also coached a girl's ringette team. As soon as I turned five years old I was allowed to join up. I had never really heard of the game called ringette but wanted to be good at it because Linda was good at it. It turned out ringette was kind of like hockey light, but only girls played it. It wasn't as much fun as hockey looked like it was, but I kept going to practices because my mom had spent all that money on skates and a helmet for me. There were barely enough girls to make one team so we never got to play a real game, we mostly skated around and practiced stopping. That's the truth, and also a metaphor. Some of the girls came in figure skates, but not me.

One day Don Dixon showed up early at practice and watched us run a passing drill for a while. He told Linda after practice that I was already a better skater than half the boys on the Squirts team he coached and so did I want to come and play with the boys? he asked.

I didn't even have to think before I said yes. My mom said hold on, she had to talk it over with my dad, who was only half listening because he was reading that book *Shogun* and it was a super good book he said, and my mom said yes, I guess, you can play hockey, but be careful out there. Linda taught me how to do a slap shot and told me never to skate with my head down. I was the only girl playing in the Whitehorse Minor Hockey League for eleven years after that. I made it all the way up to junior hockey. Left wing.

When I turned sixteen they wouldn't let me play hockey with the boys anymore. I was now a legal liability, they told my parents, and the minor hockey league just couldn't afford that kind of insurance, and besides, what if I got hurt, the boys were so much bigger now, plus body-checking. Come and play on the women's team with us, Linda said, and so I did.

That was how I met Donna Doucette, who played defense and worked as a bartender at the Kopper King on the Alaska Highway. Donna Doucette wore her long brown hair in a whip-like braid that swung between her shoulder blades when she skated back hard for the puck. I think I pretty much fell in love with Donna Doucette the first time I saw her spit perfectly through the square holes in the face mask on her helmet. She just curled her tongue into a tube and horked unapologetically right through her mask. It shot like a bullet, about fifteen feet, straight out onto the ice. I had never seen a woman do anything like that before, I could only imagine the back-of-the-head slap my gran would lay on me if I ever dared to spit anywhere in public, much less turn it into an art form like Donna Doucette did.

I remember hearing her playing fastball one midnight sunny summer evening; I was playing softball on the field next to the women's league. All the women on my hockey team played ball together in the summer; like serious fast pitch, they were not fooling around. Hockey was for sport but fast pitch was for keeps. Donna Doucette played shortstop and would spare no skin to make a catch, and she spat all over the goddamn place out there on the field too, and cussed and catcalled. Hey batter batta batta swing batta batta. I remember her in silhouette, bobbing back and forth on the toes of her cleats, all backlit by the sun and gum a-chew, a mouthy shadow, punching the pocket of her gloved hand with her red-nailed fingertips coiled into a fist.

That's the thing about Linda and Donna. They weren't like me. Linda wore sapphire studs in her ears and a red red dress to our Christmas party. Donna swore and stole third base wearing what my mother claimed to be too much eye makeup for daylight hours, which even back then I thought was kind of harsh, it being summer in the Yukon and it never really getting dark and all.

Donna and Linda. My memories of them are sharp, hyper-focused. I was paying attention to every detail of them, I was searching them for clues to who I wanted to be, but I already knew I couldn't be like them. I wanted something else. Something close to what they had. They hinted at a kind of freedom, a kind of just not giving a fuck what anyone said about them that made me want things I didn't know the words for.

Theresa Turner drove her two-stroke dirt bike to school every day we were in grade eleven, appearing out of the willows and trailing a tail of dust as she gunned the throttle and skidded to a stop by the tree line at the edge of our high school parking lot. She would dismount and stomp her kickstand down with the heel of her buckled biker boot and shake her mane of mahogany ringlets loose from under her helmet and strut in her skin-tight Levi 501s past the heads smoking cigarettes by the back double doors to the wood shop. Fuck you looking at? she would sneer at them. This for some reason made them blush, and pretend they weren't watching her ass swing as the door hissed shut behind her. I was old enough by then to be full-on smitten.

Carolyn O'Hara was Theresa Turner's very best friend from Cedar. Cedar was a suburb of the pulp mill town of Nanaimo where I was living with my grandmother. Theresa Turner and Carolyn O'Hara had grown up out there together and had known each other all their lives. They also knew all about all the boys from the rural working class outskirts of Nanaimo. Knew all the boys who had to skip school in the fall to bring in the hay and miss entire weeks in the spring when the lambs came.

They knew all about the boys with the jean jacket vests with ZZ Top or Judas Priest album covers recreated in ballpoint ink. Houses of the Holy. The boys whose older brothers were doing time.

Carolyn O'Hara had a necklace strung of these diamonds in the rough, these boys who would punch locker doors and prick the skin in between their forefinger and thumb and rub ink into it in the shape of a broken heart all for the love of Carolyn O'Hara. She had her brother who died in a motorcycle accident's acoustic guitar and she would play "Walk on the Wild Side" by Lou Reed at lunch. I remember her swinging her honey-brown hair in the sun in the front seat of Eddie Bartolo's midnight blue Nova with the windows rolled down and saying, "So what if I am on the rag, you asshole. I'd like to see you go to gym class and do your fucking flexed arm hang exercises if you'd been bleeding out of your ass like it's going out of goddamn style for the last three fucking days. You going to smoke that thing or pass it on, you selfish bastard?"

Carolyn O'Hara could out-swear even Theresa Turner, it's why they were the perfect pair. Carolyn O'Hara was gorgeous. Could have been a model, everybody said so, but she was very practical and took the dental hygienist's program up at the college right after we graduated.

I ran into Theresa one day about five years ago, on my way to Vancouver Island for a gig. Theresa was wearing false eyelashes and an orange reflective vest at the same time, which I thought was awesome. Hugged me hard and told me she had been working for BC Ferries for seventeen years now, doing what my gran had always said was a good, clean, union job if you liked people. Said Carolyn O'Hara had opened her own dog grooming business. A real cool place where you can drop your dog off to get groomed, or rent a big tub and wash your own dog in the back. She said they were both happy, they still kept in real good touch, in fact they were going for mani-pedis for their fortieth birthdays just next week.

Mia Telerico. Fall of 1992, she had just moved to town from Toronto. I met her in my friend's coffee shop on the Drive, she smoked Du Maurier Light King Size and I smoked Player's Light regulars. I, for reasons unexamined by me at the time, I guess I was trying to impress her, so I spontaneously leapt up and did a dramatic reading for her of *The Cat in The Hat,* and we briefly became lovers, and then, so far, life-long friends. Mia Telerico said in my kitchen one night that first winter It's E-Talian, not Eye-Talian, you sound like a redneck if you say it wrong, and then she showed me how to peel a bunch of garlic all at once by crushing it with the side of the butcher knife.

How many ways do I love Mia Telerico? I love that she refinishes furniture and owns all her own power tools and that it takes hours for her curls to dry so she has special hair-washing days, because washing her hair is like, a thing, right, and she is missing part of a finger from an accident she had cleaning the chain on her motorcycle and she is tough as nails but with the softest heart and bosom, can I even use the word "bosom" anymore? I don't know. Her hugs feel better than nearly anything is all I'm saying, and when she lets me rest my head there for a second I feel so untouchable, so unhurtable somehow, so magically protected by her soft cheek and rough hands ever capable. I called her just now and left a message asking her if it was okay if I called her a femme tomboy, how does she feel about me pinning those words on her femme tomboy, but really, all I'm trying to do here is broaden the joining, I tell her voice mail. All I want to do is honour all the femme tomboys I have ever loved, and thank them for showing me the possibilities. Anyway. Mia's father was from Malta and her mother is Italian and her dad was a janitor and her ma worked in a chocolate factory just like I Love Lucy and Ethel except less funny and for decades until it wrecked her back.

I left Mia Telerico a message but I haven't heard back yet. I hear through the grapevine that she is going through a breakup and, well, I guess I am too, and both of us, we take these things pretty hard, artist's hearts pumping just beneath the skin of our chests like they do.

The woman working at the Tim Hortons in the London airport and I just did a tattoo show-and-tell session together. Her
co-worker even helped her undo her uniform shirt and pull the
back of the collar partway down to show me the wolf on her back. It
was funny and we bonded, and then we both just stood there for a
minute, both of our shirts disheveled and unbuttoned, smiling at
each other, kind of embarrassed. I asked her where the tip jar was.
She said they had to keep it under the counter. We both agreed this
was no fair.

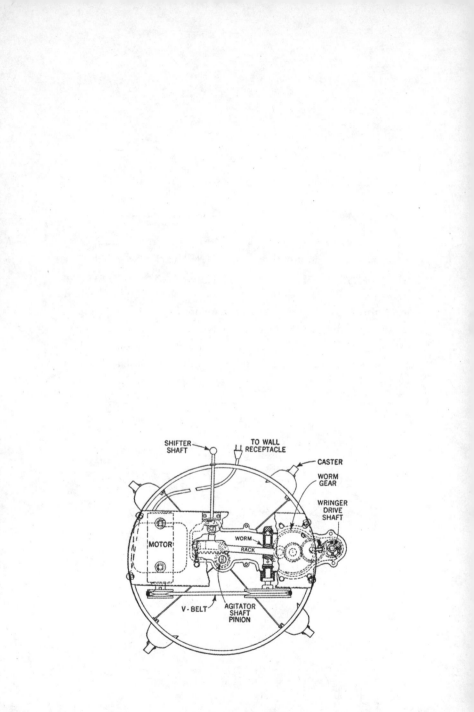

# SHOULDN'T I FEEL PRETTY?

On June 25, I received the following email:

Dear Ivan:

I was just wondering if you always knew? When did you become comfortable in your own skin? See, I always felt not quite right ... I'd put on dresses or high heels and makeup and look in the mirror and I just didn't feel right. Shouldn't I feel pretty? Why didn't I like what I saw? I'm forty-four years old and I think I've just realized that maybe girls and women's clothes weren't right for me all along. I feel stupid that it took me so long to realize what I am. It breaks my heart that it took me so long.

I don't even know where to begin to feel right, to feel good, to feel beautiful. Any tips?

I wrote this person back and told them I needed a couple of days to think about all of this. Here is my response to them:

I get these letters now. I get these letters from people who are hurting. It's a terrifying thing, the pain of a stranger. Impossible to bear it all, even on a strong day, even when the sun is shining and my back doesn't hurt and the dishes are all done.

Mostly I think people just want to know they are not alone, that they are not the only one trying to swallow and breathe around the big empty abandoned town hall their heart is echoing inside of.

Should I tell them the truth, I wonder? Do they really want to know I feel just as lost as they do, some days? Are two lost people any better off when they find each other?

Instead I make a cup of strong black tea with canned milk and one brown sugar and I sit down to find the trail into the truth of these things in the only way I have ever known how. By collecting up words, and then walking around with them in my mouth, words arguing between my ears, words leaving my heart in great lumps and then lining up in single file in my lungs to get said out loud.

Let me write about September 1974, when I first started kindergarten and my mom cut me a deal that I could wear pants to school every other day. Which meant a dress every day that wasn't a pants day. The night before a wear a dress day I would have bad dreams, I would have these panicked dreams about boys waiting under the backless wooden stairs that led into the portable trailer next to the school where my kindergarten class was held. Sweating fear-stained dreams of laughing boys looking up my skirt, and I couldn't even kick them properly because have you ever tried to do a high kick in a long dress? The harder you kick the faster your one raised leg pulls your other leg out from under you. Hot tears on my cheek and my bare thigh torn up by the gravel. I am sure I know many people who have perfected a technique to account for the high kick in a long dress phenomena, but I never did. I just dragged myself to school for months, every other day afraid and exhausted, until my mom took pity on me and bought me two more pairs of brown corduroys on sale at the old Bay in the Qwanlin Mall. She sighed and put them into the third drawer of my dresser with a cutting look in my direction because I had disappointed her again.

And so began a lifetime of hating most of my clothes.

I spent much of my early years shirtless in the summers, in most old pictures of me I am smiling and sunburned from the waist up, my pant legs stuffed into black rubber boots with red-brown toes, good for standing in the shallow water catching tadpoles or spin-casting. Until that tourist man from Texas camped two sites down from us called me young man and my mom corrected him because I was seven years old and we were standing in the line-up for the ladies' showers. Go and put a t-shirt on, she told me, and leave it on this time, I am not going to tell you again.

I used to be mad at her for squeezing me into everything, but I grew out of it. I know now that she was just worried about me. I wish that she had named what I saw in her eyes when she looked at me back then, I wish that she had called it fear. Because all those years I mistook that fear for shame, and that mistake has cost us both so much.

I like to think that I suffered the same as every teenage girl does in her changing body. I don't think that trans people hold the monopoly or wrote the only book on hating our bodies, and even if we did win at this contest I wouldn't want the prize anyway. Describe the pain on a scale from one to ten the doctor always says, but no one knows where zero sits. Did I hate my tiny tits any more than the beginnings of these hips? Hard to say, really.

Shouldn't I feel pretty?

I can count the times on one hand when I did, and even those moments were fleeting, always collapsing as soon as I moved or

breathed, my elbows were too sharp, my knees never folded right, my shoulders were too wide, my all of me was lacking a certain kind of grace.

Why didn't I like what I saw? Probably because I felt like nobody else did.

I kissed my first girl in 1988. She was a jazz singer. She wasn't queer, she said, she just fell in love with me by accident, and I said I didn't mind when her parents came to town and she introduced me as her roommate. I told her I understood, because I did.

I was a baby butch who had not ever heard the word and so didn't know what to call my own self until I first read that word out loud in 1992 in the back stacks of Little Sister's bookstore. I wore second-hand army boots three sizes too big and cut my own hair with clippers and met what I didn't know at the time was my first femme lover and bought my first necktie and she called me handsome and that one word handsome made up for two decades of knowing I was never really all that pretty.

The first trans man I ever met in real life was still a lesbian separatist at the time, who cornered me up against the wall at the Lotus Club and chastised me for wearing a mascara moustache out to the bar on women-only night. I see him now sometimes on Commercial Drive sporting his full and luscious beard, but we talk about other things, and I forgive, but I don't forget how lonely I felt that night.

In 1995 I started to bind my breasts. First with Saran wrap, then Ace bandages, then by wearing a double front compression shirt. Flattening them and hiding them under my clothes didn't make me hate them any less, but it did make it easier to look in the mirror, and leave my apartment.

In 2008 I was about to turn forty and my body was becoming something I could not even recognize. Every twenty-eight days my tits would swell and ache and get bigger. My hips were doing things I had long admired in others but could not reconcile with my own flesh and frame. I started to seriously lift weights.

Somewhere in the sweat and ache and muscle, I carved a new shape for myself that made more sense to me. You should do more cardio and lift less weight, my mom told me when I was home for a visit and she saw me bulging in a t-shirt at her kitchen table. Don't let yourself get any bigger, she said. Don't get any more tattoos. I took this as a sign, and really buckled down on the bicep curls. Felt more like myself.

I wish I could say that I learned to be truly comfortable in this body of mine before I finally had top surgery in 2013, but that would be a lie. I try every day to not let it break my heart that it took me so long. I was forty-four years old and it breaks my heart that it took me so long.

When did I know, you ask me? Since always, I guess. Probably just like you have always known, somewhere in you, I know you have always known.

I look at pictures of shirtless me at five years old, and I can see the shape of my now flat chest foreshadowed in my tiny frame even back then. I like my body now, from about the bellybutton up, and most days that is almost enough to say I nearly feel comfortable in my own skin. I almost feel close to right. I love the shape of my ass when I am naked, but not so much when I am trying on dark denim skinny jeans in hipster stores that sprung up where greasy spoon diners and glove factories used to be.

I am grateful that I can now afford a well-cut shirt and a real silk tie, and a tailor. A good haircut once a month. A fancy jacket with these cool elbows on it. I know these things make me lucky. These things make me feel more confident, more myself, but they don't make me. I made me. This world made me. Struggle and fear and sweat and work and words made me. Did any of it come too late? I don't think so. Here I am, and I think everything happened when it happened nearly exactly how it needed to go down and now I am here, and I feel handsome and strong, and that, well, that is a beautiful thing.

Thank you for writing. I hope you are lucky like me. I hope you get this letter and it helps you somehow, helps you lift your chin and your eyes. I hope you learn to stand up full inside of yourself, I hope you one day wear yourself on your sleeve, on your French cuffs, on your chest like a medal of honour.

You are going to need to find your freak family. Your misfit soldiers and their weirdo army. Keep your eyes open. That little boy at school that the bigger kids are picking on. Ask him if he has a secret name he wants you to call him. Tell him yours. Tell him he is beautiful. Tell him you see all the ways that he is strong like you and it has nothing to do with throwing a ball. Tell him you will be there at the other end of the string between you, listening into that tin can if he needs you.

The world will be full of messages telling you to be something other than what you are. Telling you that you are too skinny or too fat or too dark or too hairy. Too poor for pretty. Low fat hide your belly quick loss how to love less and find a man maps to time machines that only ever go backward. The magazines are full of this nonsense.

Save those magazines. They can be very useful. You can duct tape them over your jeans to make shin pads for street hockey and quick, cheap armour for fencing or general swordplay. Touché.

Clothespin a playing card to the spokes of your new bike and make some noise. Keep their good little girl cocoon in a mason jar with holes in the lid and let the moths out when they hatch. Leave fist marks and boot prints and lipstick stains all over their glass ceilings. Leave all closet doors open everywhere. Make a habit of this.

You don't have to look a certain way to be a tomboy. Don't let anyone tell you that, ever, and please don't find that here in my words. Tomboy thrums in your heart. It's in your head. It's what is holding your spine in place. It can't be hidden by a haircut. It's not about nail polish or not. It's running right now in your veins. If it is in you, you already know. Tomboy blood is so much bigger than the outside of you.

Kid at the grocery store today to his father:

"Why does that man have those big earrings like that?" He is referring to a tattooed dude with those huge plug-type ear hoops.

Dad to his son: "I guess they are his way of expressing himself."

Kid thinks about this for a second. "Like how Mommy does her karate?"

Dad smiles and says, "Yeah. Sort of exactly like that."

# DEAR PATRICIA

You had me fourteen days before your twentieth birthday. I was your first of two girls. It was a story, that whole spring and summer. You had just been crowned Rendezvous Queen, the belle of the ball of our winter festival, on February 28, and then found out you were pregnant. With me. They took back your tiara and your fur coat and blue satin sash, and you were married on March 5. The sponsors couldn't have a pregnant princess. I was born in August. Grandpa Al said ... you know what? It doesn't matter what he said about you back then, not anymore.

The pictures contain all the evidence of me, right from the very start. Me standing naked in his work boots. Me in my hockey gear, with a fishing rod. You with your hair in a perfect beehive, even when we were camping. I know I was never the daughter you dreamt of. Did you even dream of daughters? I've never asked you. I know you never got to go to fashion school like you wanted. You used to sew our clothes from patterns, you were good at it. You made your own wedding dress. It was rust coloured. I don't know if you wanted kids, but still you showed up, picked me up after practice, wrote a letter to the school so I could take shop instead of sewing. Band-Aids, birthdays. Santa had your handwriting. Always it was you. The house was always clean. I don't know how you did it all. He was more like a cool uncle that just dropped in. Your father is still at work, you would say. Thank you for starting supper, you would say. I would fall asleep to the sound of the clothes dryer still spinning, into the night.

I remember when you and he separated. He was gone somewhere, I don't remember where, and he left you to pack up the house when it sold. I showed up to help you put stuff into boxes. I had just gotten a fresh haircut. You look just like him in this light, you said, and I held both of your hands in mine and felt guilty about the shape of my own cheekbones.

I get my work ethic from you, and you get it from gran. We all get it from gran, you tell me on the phone. Your mother. She weighed almost nothing when she died. Her first job was in a cardboard box-making factory. That was where she crushed all eight fingers in the corrugating machine. She was five-foot-six when she first came to Canada, it said so in her immigration papers, and four-foot-ten at the end. What does a life of hard work cost a woman? Eight inches off of her back, you tell me on the phone. You are talking to me from inside your condo, and I am listening on the other end of the phone line, sitting in mine.

I remember the first time I saw that picture of you in front of the green house on Sixth Avenue and Lambert, I'm ashamed now to admit that I felt a little shame. Those old pictures. Telling all the stories you have left behind you. Black and white dirt road and the humble clothes. Now, I am older and I have replaced that word shame with others, closer to strength, closer to gratitude, and to pride.

I never prayed or confessed anything to the priest because he was your older brother and I knew some of his old stories, too. Uncle Father Dave. Your brother Father Dave. He died on my birthday four years ago. I hope he finally found his salvation. I hope he was forgiven. I don't remember ever praying to god to make me a boy. I guess I just wanted for things to be different for girls.

You gave my little sister your name as her middle name. I'm glad for this, because it might have hurt you even more when I changed all of my names. I would have hated to have been given your name, and then have had to discard it like I did my surname. You said my birth name came from a book and it meant warrior woman, and you called my sister Caroline. Caroline Patricia.

I'm so glad for the blood of yours that is inside of me. I love hearing your laugh tinkle and flash above all of the noise of all of us in one house together. You have let your hair grow out silver. Your bangs are long and you tuck them behind your ear with one finger before you pour the hot water for tea or bend to pick up your great-niece. I inherited your good teeth and love of a clean kitchen. I think of you whenever I leave perfect vacuum marks in the carpet in the bedroom.

If I had to hold only one memory of us all together when we were young, because you really were young with us, it would be Saturday mornings in the new house on Grove Street, after we had finished the housework and you would put a record on and me and Carrie would take turns standing on the tops of your feet and you would dance us around in circles on the freshly vacuumed carpet. Supertramp's *Crime of the Century* and America's "A Horse With No Name" and Cat Stevens' *Tea for the Tillerman* and always the Beatles. The sun cutting through the room in a yellow stripe behind you, and you would say it is time to do these windows again, lookit the fingerprints I'll do it in a minute.

You knew the boogie and the hand jive and the box step and that one dance where you hold your nose and pretend you are going underwater, what's it called? I knew this meant there was a time before us and this house and that job and the lawn and the laundry when you were freer and could play records in the living room and learn dances that had real moves and names. Dad would never dance, if he was home he would sit on the couch and smoke. That look on his face.

It didn't matter. We had you.

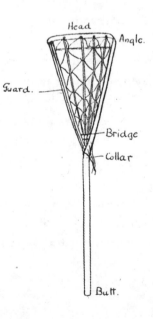

# HOW TO BUILD YOUR VERY OWN UNICORN TRAP

My uncle Rob tells this story about me, about the first time he ever met me. He was young, in his twenties, and had been living and surfing and romancing New Zealand and Australia for some time and had just returned home to the Yukon. He walked up the unpaved street on the just-punched-into-the-pine-trees cul-de-sac my dad had built our first house on. He knocked on our front door and I answered. I was almost four years old. He stuck out his hand and said, "You must be my niece. I'm your Uncle Rob." I nodded perfunctorily and shook his hand with my right hand. I was hiding my left hand behind my back, as he tells it. "Do you want to see a dead gopher?" I asked him. Always game, he replied, "Why yes, I would love to see a dead gopher." So I pulled my left hand out from behind my back and triumphantly held up a road-killed and flattened and sundried dead gopher for him to peruse. Of course, I was extremely proud of myself.

I was one of the lucky ones. One of the lucky tomboys who, for the most part, was loved and allowed to pretty much be myself. At home, at least, if not at school or on the streets. Some of us are not so lucky. Some of us have that difference squeezed or pounded or prayed out of us. But still here we are, scraped up and sometimes more than a little scarred, but still. We survive. We have survived. When I look back, I know what helped me through. Skills. Knowing, asking, learning, practicing, and dreaming about how to do stuff. Even if girls weren't supposed to be able to. Even though I sometimes had to fight to pick up that hammer or hatchet or helmet or handsaw. Even if it was unbecoming and no boy or man would ever want me. Even when I did manage to be good at something, I was reminded that yeah, I was pretty good at that, for a girl. Even if it was all so unlady-like.

I also had to believe in magic. I had to believe in the northern lights, I had to believe in the smell of dry Yukon dirt just before the first raindrops fell, I had to believe that I could jump into the deep end and ski down that hill and that one day I could make even my dad proud of having a daughter like me. I had to believe that everything would get easier.

So in the interest of promoting this skills-based approach to magic, I'm now about to teach you a little trick I learned back home when I was a kid.

These are directions for building your very own cruelty-free, non-leg-hold unicorn trap. Results may vary, and of course there is no way to guarantee that there are still any unicorns living in or visiting your area. But if you are patient, and lucky, and follow equal parts directions and your heart, it just might work for you. You might just trap a unicorn.

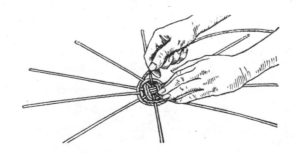

## STEP ONE: THE CIRCLE

You have to find a quiet place in the forest. It is a well-known fact that unicorns do not like the smell of automobile exhaust, so you should look for a spot that is far away from roads or highways.

Once you have found your spot in the forest, you must make sure it is free of litter and debris, especially cigarette butts. Unicorns are allergic to smoke. Next, you need to collect between thirty and forty stones, all about the size of an apple. Place the stones in a large circle. Stand in the centre of the circle and feel good about what you have built. My witchy friends tell me this is called "casting the circle."

This next part is very important. Once you have cast the circle, you cannot think or say anything mean or nasty while you are inside it. Unicorns can smell cruelty on a person from a great distance, even lateral aggression, and they will not come anywhere near your circle if it smells mean to them. This is especially important if you bring more than one human into the circle. Everybody has to be kind to each other while in or near the circle, or it will never work. For example, if you laugh at your friend because they have to wear glasses or their pants are too short, or if anyone pinches anyone non-consensually, a unicorn can smell it and will avoid the area, sometimes for months after the incident.

## STEP TWO: THE BAIT

Not very many people know this trick, so don't go blabbing it to just anyone. I learned this from my grandmother, who learned it from her grandmother, who learned it from a lady in her square-dancing group. Unicorns have a sweet tooth. They cannot resist a jam and honey sandwich, especially with the crusts cut off. No butter, just jam and not too much honey, or the bread will get soggy. Make it at home and wrap it up so it stays fresh. This is your bait. Do not eat your bait. Make your own sandwich, just in case you get hungry.

## STEP THREE: BE PATIENT

Place the jam and honey sandwich on a large stone or a stump in the middle of your circle of stones. Sit down quietly and wait. You should bring a book or some art supplies and paper, as it could take a while. Sometimes it can take days. Look at this time as an opportunity to get some reading done, or to paint a picture. Avoid playing video games or texting, as these devices have been known to scare off a unicorn, especially the older ones. Older unicorns have longer horns, of course, and know more about poetry and folk music.

If you are lucky and a unicorn enters your circle, do not make any loud noises or sudden movements. Just sit still and let the unicorn approach the jam and honey sandwich. Unicorns have often had bad luck when interacting with humans in the past, so don't take it too personally if the unicorn has trust issues with you at first. Give the unicorn time to sniff the sandwich and have a little nibble.

While the unicorn is enjoying their sandwich, begin to speak to it in a slow, gentle whisper. Do not attempt to touch it, as it will bolt, and probably never come back. Just whisper to it gently. Tell the unicorn how magnificent it is. How shiny its coat looks today. Whisper that it has the longest eyelashes you have ever seen. This is the trick, you see, they have a weakness for praise. As long as you are saying nice things to that unicorn, it will be unable to leave the circle you have cast. It simply cannot walk away when someone is telling it how gorgeous it is. How handsome. What shiny, rippling haunches it has. It cannot help but continue to listen. Don't stop. In fact, try not to pause much at all. It will eventually fall under your spell.

If you run out of things to say, you can also sing love songs to it, as love songs will work too, as will almost anything by the Beatles, especially their older stuff.

Again, do not attempt to touch the unicorn. Do not take pictures. Not only do cameras scare most unicorns off, nothing will show up in the pictures anyway. It's a unicorn thing that scientists cannot explain. Of course, this works out well for the unicorns. They want people to think they are just make believe.

This last bit is the most important part of all: You must not attempt to physically trap, tie down, or otherwise capture the unicorn. Unicorns live most of the time in another dimension, and only visit ours rarely. Capturing one permanently is impossible, as the unicorn, if threatened in any way, will simply escape to another time-space continuum. And tenderhearted and delicate as they are, that particular unicorn might never risk visiting us in this dimension ever again. Please do not ruin someone else's chances of experiencing a unicorn sighting here on planet Earth.

Again, this is only a plan for a unicorn trap, and comes with no guarantees that it will result in an actual unicorn sighting, or temporary compliment trapping. The last recorded unicorn trapping happened in Newfoundland just last summer, when two twin sisters and their downstairs neighbour held a unicorn in their magic circle on the beach for nearly three hours by singing its praises in three-part harmony that they learned in choir class.

There are no guarantees, but the worst thing that will happen is that you and maybe a few friends will spend some time in the forest or in nature being kind to each other and perhaps reading or drawing, after having picked up some litter and collecting magic rocks, so really, you have nothing to lose.

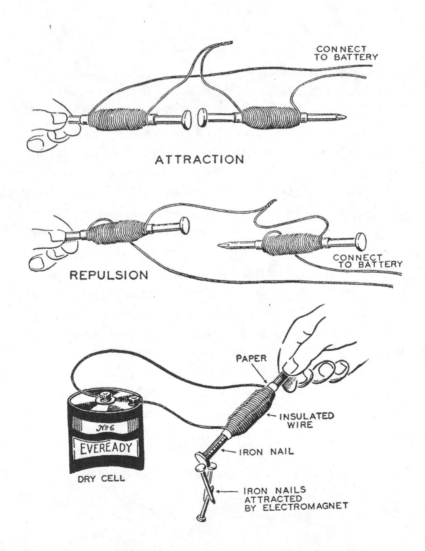

CONNECT TO BATTERY

ATTRACTION

REPULSION

CONNECT TO BATTERY

PAPER

INSULATED WIRE

IRON NAIL

No 6

EVEREADY

DRY CELL

IRON NAILS ATTRACTED BY ELECTROMAGNET

Autocorrect keeps trying to change the word butches to "but he's." Back off, autocorrect. We're dismantling the binary here. Step aside and let us work.

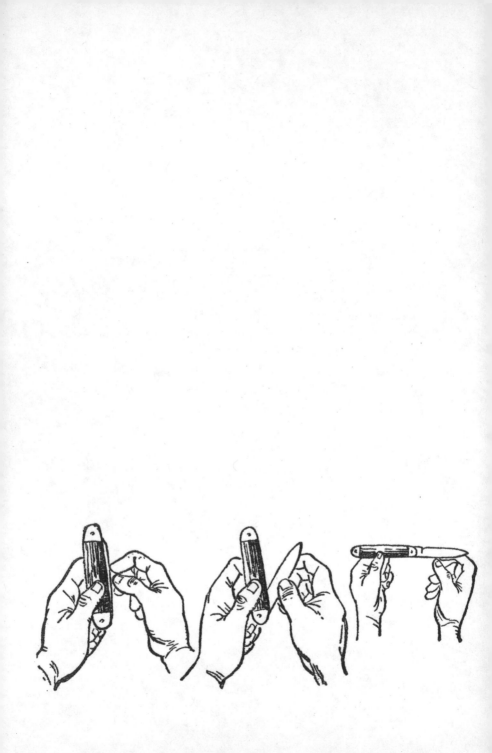

# BE CAREFUL IN THERE

So I know how it goes. You are eight years old and it's Saturday morning and your mom dropped you off at your Brownies meeting at the old community centre and it was the Kozchek twins' birthday so there was cake and red juice and who can resist that red juice, right? It's so good. So you drank three glasses of the stuff. And now you have karate at noon and you have to get changed from your stupid brown skirt and uniform shirt and into your *karategi* and you can never be late for karate because it's all about the discipline, right, and also you have to seriously pee because three glasses of red juice. So you duck quietly, you slip quickly into the women's change room and it is full of the yoga ladies all fresh and sweaty from their class and when you walk in one of them squints her eyes at you and makes a face and says, "Excuse me, young man?" and then all of a sudden twenty-nine pairs of yoga lady eyes are on you all at once and you feel like you don't belong in there at all even though you know in your heart that you do.

Or at least you know you belong in the women's change room a little bit more than you belong in the men's room. After all, you're only what, eight years old? An eight-year-old tomboy alone in the men's room? This could be even more dangerous than yoga lady eyes.

So there you are with twenty-nine yoga ladies all stopped staring at you, even though doesn't anyone notice you are wearing an actual Brownie's uniform? Isn't that some kind of a clue right there? Can't a girl cut her hair short these days? Even though your friend Joanne has her hair nearly as short as yours but for some reason this type of stuff never happens to her. Nobody calls her young man all the time and they let her pee in peace. What's the deal?

But you are eight years old so you don't have much to say yet about your more nuanced placement on the in-betweens of the gender binary, all you really know is that you are going to turn around and you are going to go outside and you are going to pee in the willow bushes by the green belt next to the parking lot because this is easier.

Then you will get changed for karate behind a green minivan and hope that there are no perverts lurking around or rubbernecked boys trying to catch a glimpse when their moms pick them up after hockey practice or Beavers, right? All you know is there is no bathroom door with the silhouette of someone who looks anything like you on it.

And how do I know all of this? Because I've been there. I want you to know you are not alone. You feel like you are the only one in Moose Jaw or Creston or Canmore or Prince George or Whitehorse or Fort Smith or Bishop's Falls, and well, maybe you are. But I promise you that you are not alone. I'm here. I'm here and I see you. I feel you. I was you, and I still am you.

It's not you, it's them. It really is. And those boxes, those binaries, those bathroom signs, those rigid roles, they hurt them too, they do, they carve away at their souls and secret desires and self-esteem and believable dreams and possible wardrobes and acceptable careers just like they do ours, just it's harder for them to tell it's happening on account of no one is hassling them in the bathrooms every other day about it. They somehow just fit better in those boxes, so they can't see what fitting has cost them, not like we can.

I know what you are thinking, and you are right. This all could be solved with a single-stall, locking, gender-neutral washroom in all schools and so-called public buildings. It could. It seems simple to you, because it is. We all have gender-neutral bathrooms at home. We just call them bathrooms.

You will ask for a safer place to pee and they will say things like we are talking about this next month in a meeting, and we are weighing all of our options here, or, we are busy assessing whether this is a need or a want, or they will tell you that it is too late or too expensive or against their religion and besides, why can't you just  be more like all the other little girls or boys? If you could just be different, they will say, or is it less different, then none of us would have to accommodate any of you.

I know, it's really hard not to just hear it like somehow you just don't matter as much, and sometimes it might feel better if they just came right out and just fessed up that your safety and your right to have a place to get changed for gym class just doesn't matter as much as theirs does.

You will be asked to be patient, and you will be, because you have no other choice. Real change takes time, they will say, and can't you ask more politely? Your anger will not help anyone listen or understand, they will tell you. But in the meantime, where do you pee, you wonder? Your bladder can't wait and you've got karate at noon.

So. Here is some of what I have learned to do, over my forty-seven years so far of bathroom troubles:

Head for the first stall closest to the door. Smile and make eye contact if you choose the ladies room, avoid eye contact if you go with the men's room. Try to act like you belong there, even though they have made it quite clear that you do not. Try not to act scared.

Try to remember to breathe.

Engage your superhuman powers. Try your cloaking device, your force field of invisibility, or your gift for shifting shapes. Open the eyes you have in the back of your head. All of these powers are somewhat diminished under fluorescent lights, and lowered if you need a snack or have your period, but your many superpowers can and do help.

Keep smiling and be polite if anyone speaks to you in there. I know this one is hard, especially if they are yelling at you or telling you to get out, or gasping or gawking or whispering, or calling security on you. It's not fair that you have to remain calm when they are being rude, or calling you names, or hitting you with their purse, but trust me, things will go better for you if you can manage to stay polite and smiling. Forgive yourself immediately if and when you grow impatient with them.

Also, try finding a bathroom, men's or women's, on a quieter floor, or a different part of the building. Remember it for next time, too. Of course a lonely bathroom in a deserted part of the building could be dangerous in a whole other bunch of ways, so weigh your options and trust your intuition.

You could also try bringing a friend in with you. My cousin and I do this thing sometimes, she has very long curly hair and good nails and as we walk in she asks me in a very loud feminine voice if I have a tampon in my purse she can borrow. Sometimes this works, but maybe if you are only five years old you could change the wording up a little? You are going to have to learn to think on your feet.

I want you to know how it hurts me inside that you are only five or eight or thirteen or thirty-five or eighty-nine years old and you are already, or still, or perpetually having to navigate all of this just to go to Brownies or karate or math class or the doctor's office or college or the movies. At least we are safe in airplane bathrooms. If we can make it through those new machines at the security gate.

Do I sound tired? Maybe today I really am. Maybe I just got off of the road and I had to pee in a lot of strange bathrooms. Maybe I'm forty-seven years old and sick to death of smiling and being polite about it all. Maybe change feels too slow and too far and too fallible to me today. But know this: it's them, not you, and I see you. There is nothing wrong with you.

And one day, you, my little friend, will tell an eight-year-old tomboy or girlboy or other brave and magical gender inventor about how there used to be only two kinds of bathrooms to choose from, and you had to fit yourself into a box to safely go into one, and your little friend will laugh and not believe you. They will laugh and say how ridiculous, because then where would someone like me go to get changed for karate? That couldn't be, they will say, and you will laugh too, because they are right. That just couldn't be.

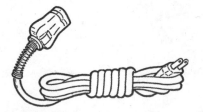

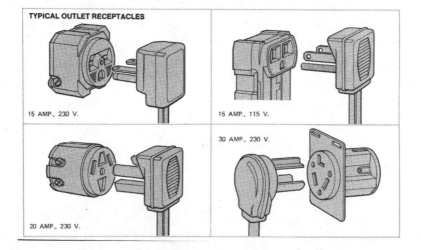

**TYPICAL OUTLET RECEPTACLES**

15 AMP., 230 V.

15 AMP., 115 V.

20 AMP., 230 V.

30 AMP., 230 V.

# WILL YOU COME WITH ME?

**E**
All right boys, listen to me
**B**
All right girls, here's the scene
**E**
It's a beautiful night (yes yes)
**B**
The stars are out (yes yes)
**E**
I'm on a date with my baby
**B**
And then I get that feeling
**A**                                **B**
You know the one I'm meaning (tell it tell it tell it tell it)
So I say
**B**
Can you check out the bathroom situation with me?

**C#m**
Are you in the wrong place?
                   **F#m**
Look how you are dressed
What do you expect?

**C#m**
Are you in the wrong place?
                              **F#m**
Look how you are dressed
What do you expect?
        **G#m**
The people say shriek
**B**
You're such a freak


**B**
I can hold it, I can hold it, I can hold it


**E**
Maybe I can wait till I get home
**C#m**
Maybe I can wait till I get on the plane
**G#m**
Baby can you check out the situation
**A**                    **B**
This happens every day


**C#m**
Will you come with me baby?
                        **G#m   A**
Will you come with me
**C#m**
Will you come with me baby?
**G#m   A   E**
Will you come with me

All right boys, listen to me
All right girls, here's the scene
It's a beautiful night (yes yes)
The stars are out (yes yes)

Are you in the wrong place?
Look how you are dressed
What do you expect?

Are you in the wrong place?
Look how you are dressed
What do you expect?

The people say shriek
You're such a freak

I can hold it, I can hold it, I can hold it

Maybe I can wait til I get home
Maybe I can wait til I get on the plane
Better bring my baby in with me
Safety in numbers then

Will you come with me, baby?
Will you come with me?
Will you come with me, baby?
Will you come with me?

Woman in the women's bathroom at the ferry terminal: "Um, excuse me, sir …?" Me: "Could you please wait until after I pee to tell me I'm in the wrong bathroom? I just worked all day and then drove for two hours." Her: "Of course. Absolutely." And she did wait. She waited by the sink until I came out of the stall, and then she apologized to me at length. Said she was sorry, and that her grandson was exploring his gender identity and that she should know better. I asked her how her grandson was doing. She said he was a beautiful person who played piano and was a great artist, too. She said she loved him or her very much. She thanked me for my patience. I thanked her for her honesty and good heart. Asked her to please give my best wishes to her grandchild. Then we smiled at each other and went back to our vehicles.

Ratchet set. Grease nipples. Plaid. Harris tweed. Cufflinks. Suede. Cedar shavings. Solid teak end tables. Drill press. Oblique muscles. Coveralls. Pocketknife. Pocket square. Roadmaps. Hatchet. Hand saw. Handkerchief. Haberdashery. Remote control. Control. Power. Power steering. Swim trunks. Button down. Plain brown belt. Drum kit. Rock. Rock hammer. Level. Chisel. Chiseled. Three-piece suit, three-way switch wiring diagram. Collars stays, razor strop, and chivalry.

None of these words have a gender.

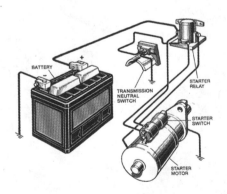

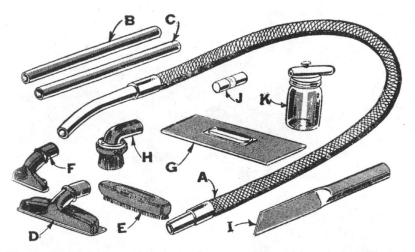

**Fig. 4.**—Typical vacuum cleaner attachments used for a wide variety of cleaning tasks. In the illustration (A) represents hose assembly; (B) and (C) extension wands; (D) floor nozzle; (E) wall brush; (F) upholstery nozzle and swivel assembly; (G) floor polisher; (H) dusting brush; (I) crevice tool and demother; (J) moth repellant; (K) sprayer.

# WHIPPER SNAPPER

I never saw them touch much, my parents. If I ever walked into the room and his hands were on her hips, he dropped them. Looked out the window or at the floor. They never said out loud that touching each other was a bad thing, but somewhere along the way it seeped into me somehow that it was. Something you didn't do in public. Something private.

Like, really private.

My uncle John had this girlfriend, named Cathy. I've written about her before, about the time she broke her leg so bad the bone poked through her shin and she barely even cried, hardly at all. About how she taught me how to ride a horse, how to get right back on when you get bucked off. Dirt between your teeth and tears still in your eyes. I knew it was a metaphor for something bigger even back then. I knew she was teaching me something I was going to need later.

What I'm thinking about tonight is her hair. How she kept it wound tight in a braid most of the time, but how this one night when her and my uncle were still building that house out on the hot springs road, she let her hair all down, perched on a stool at the end of the table, which was really just a sheet of plywood screwed to two sawhorses. The walls were still bare studs and pink fiberglass insulation covered in vapour barrier and the whole place smelled like pine sap and sawdust and the fire burning in the stone fireplace, and well, if there are any better smells than that out there then I don't know them.

Cathy had just gotten out of the shower and she shook her wet hair all out and it came right down to the backs of her knees. Like

Rapunzel, I remember thinking, only way cooler. My Aunt Cathy would never need rescuing. She would figure out a way to stay out of the locking tower.

Her hair was browny gold and rippling, like a long mane, and she held two bobby pins in her mouth and hummed along to Janis Joplin on the dusty radio on the windowsill and handed my uncle John a wide hairbrush and he took it. Just took it and started brushing her hair like he did this all the time, long even strokes from the crown of her head nearly right down to the bare plywood floor.

I remember feeling like I was witnessing something I shouldn't be there for, that I should turn and leave the room or they should stop, but it just kept happening and I couldn't take my eyes off of them. Couldn't stop watching this simple but beautiful thing. A man brushing a woman's hair. A woman that he loved. His chapped wide carpenter hands suddenly so tender. So sure.

I had never seen anything like it in my life. I love the smell of wet long hair and fresh shampoo to this day. I sometimes roll that memory around in my mouth like a smooth round stone whenever John says something crass at my grandmother's kitchen table these days. I use that image of him to chase his cruel words out of my ears. I remember this better him, and it helps me keep my mouth shut, because there is no sense fighting with him, it just upsets my grandmother and she's turning ninety-six and doesn't need the headache.

Cathy had a horse, and John loved her and built a pasture for her to keep her horse in so he could keep her there in that house with him.

He built her a little shack in one corner of that pasture, with a dusty window and a workbench and hooks for her saddle and tack and gear. It smelled like sunshine and dust and horse in there, and sounded like bees buzzing lazy in the long grass just outside.

It was the height of summer in the Yukon, early July, when the sun just dipped behind the mountains for a couple of hours and it never really got truly dark. A lawn could grow a foot in a week under that much sun if you watered it even a little bit, and you could tell who was new in town because they had packing blankets taped up over the windows in their bedrooms so they could sleep.

I was born and raised in the Yukon, and didn't even have curtains on the window in my bedroom because the back of our house looked over nothing but bush and pine trees and there was no one out there to look in, and I could sleep all night with the midnight sun shining and the lights on, too. Still can to this day.

We probably had Lipton noodle soup from a box for lunch, with grilled cheese sandwiches on white bread with a dollop of ketchup to dip them in. Or maybe Kraft dinner or ravioli from a can. I don't remember where my sister was.

I was out in the front yard of John and Cathy's place, throwing the ball for Rube, John's old golden retriever. The sun baked the dirt driveway and the air smelled like pinesap. Eventually Rube dropped the filthy tennis ball and flopped on his side in the pine needles in the shade under the front porch.

I creaked open the door to Cathy's shed and walked into the dusty fingers of light streaming through the four-paned window over the workbench. There was a bullwhip hanging in a coil on a nail half-pounded into a wall stud. I had never seen her hit a horse with it, but I had watched her swing and crack it in the air many times, her boot heels dragging half-moons in the dirt and the muscles in her shoulders rolling underneath her faded denim shirt. Smiling.

I took it down and the coils fell to the plywood floor. It felt almost alive, like a leather snake.

I stepped out into the corral, squinting into the sun.

It was way too big for me, and I had no clue how to use it, but I played with it for at least an hour, trying to flick the seed pods on the top of long grass stems, dandelion heads, a glowing brown beer bottle, a stone. I got to almost feel it crack a couple times, felt the whip extend out of the flick of my wrist and coil back towards me like a breathing thing.

My elbow started to ache and the sun beat down and still I swung the whip in a giant circle above my head, and then tried and tried and tried cracking it into all that pale blue northern sky.

I could feel the whip summoning the strength in my scrawny arm and pulling my right foot forward as it extended. I could feel my body starting to listen to the whip. My bones and muscles gathering back the energy of its length as it cut through the air with a seductive swish. The whip rallying itself to nearly crack.

And then the tip of my right ear exploded in fire. The kind of pain that makes you forget until you feel your knees hit the dirt and all the air is stolen out of you. That kind of pain where you forget even to cry for a minute until your brain catches up with the red hot angry of what just happened.

My hand clapped over the right side of my head and my fingers wet with red and dirt and dried grass in my mouth and the smell of horseshit. My legs kicking the rest of me in a circle of agony on the ground and a noise in my head that turned out to be me howling into my own ears.

Someone touched my shoulder, and I stopped kicking. Managed a raw breath. Looked up. Cathy was staring down at me, her long braid hanging down over one shoulder, the lines in her forehead knit in crosshairs of concern, an unlit cigarette dangling from one corner of her mouth.

"You okay, kiddo? I heard you scream and thought you chopped your own arm off or something. Nearly gave me a heart attack."

I sat up, my hand still welded to my ear. She pried it back with one hand and winced. Looked around. Spotted her six-foot long bullwhip in the grass.

"You crack yourself in the head with that thing? Youch. I've done that a couple of times. Fucking hurts, doesn't it? Right in the ear, too. Let's go inside and put something on it."

The mirror in her and John's downstairs bathroom was still fogged up from her shower. She sat me down on the toilet seat and washed the blood off of my ear and neck and both of my hands, like I was a little kid again, and I let her. She put some Polysporin on the open slice on the tip of the back of my ear, and called it my war wound.

Then we sat down at the plywood kitchen table on mismatched chairs and she poured me a glass of iced tea. The kind you make yourself by pouring boiling water over a bunch of tea bags in a glass pitcher and letting it sit out in the sun for a while and then adding your own sugar and lemon and putting it in the fridge.

She pulled up her pant leg and showed me the jagged white scar from when she broke her leg tobogganing. Then she showed me another between her thumb and forefinger, a thin line that wrapped right around the base of her thumb and traced into her palm.

"This was trying to make a willow chair. X-Acto blade. Twenty-one stitches. They had to operate to reattach the tendon."

She rolled up her sleeve and showed me a pink and wrinkled patch that ran up the side of her right forearm. "Deep fryer when I was cooking in that camp out on the Dempster highway. Hurt like a son of a bitch."

Pulled up her hair. Back of her neck on the right side, behind her ear. Shaped like a check mark. "Barbed wire fence."

Unzipped her jeans and pulled down her pants and underwear. Left hip.

"Kicked by a mare during a breeched birth. Back in Alberta. Should have heard the swearing. Me and my grandpa. Had to drive me to emergency in Calgary in the middle of a snowstorm. I was sixteen."

She smiled and put her forefinger on my chin. Tilted my head so she could look at my ear.

"It's going to leave a little scar. Coulda been worse for sure, though. Still got both of your eyes, right? Now you will remember this day forever."

She was, of course, totally right.

## BOLTS

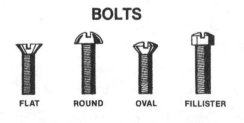

FLAT    ROUND    OVAL    FILLISTER

# STRONGER THAN THE SKIN

Under my chin. I was six years old. It happened out at the Takhini Hotsprings. It was a party for my mom's work, and I tried to jump from one tiled edge of the pool to the other deck, on an angle. I don't remember why. I didn't quite make it and cracked the bottom of my chin on the tiled edge. Head wounds. They bleed a lot. I remember someone driving my mom and I back into town to the emergency. I remember the pressure of a rough white hand towel twisted into a knot full of chipped ice from the restaurant next to the pool. They used to make such good hamburgers out there. When we got to the hospital they laid me out on the paper-covered cot. A nurse unceremoniously pulled the towel away from my chin, and my mom fainted a little from the sight of all that blood on me and had to go sit out in the hall with a cold cloth on the back of her neck while they stitched me up. Eight stitches. It looks like a pale white staple now, fatter at one end than the other.

Chickenpox scars. One on my forehead, another on my leg. I remember getting to stay home from school, but I wasn't allowed to use my Lite Brite because your eyes are very sensitive when you have the chickenpox. I don't know if this is true or not, and I also don't know if it was chickenpox or something else that I couldn't use my Lite-Brite while I was healing from it. I always blamed the chickenpox, and now I think of that Lite-Brite kit whenever my fingertip slips into the dip of that scar on my forehead. It reminds me of those craters you can see in really good pictures of the full moon.

Vaccination scars. One on my arm, another on the side of my

calf. Do they still give those to kids? Have they figured out a way not to leave a scar? I don't remember even getting them. They must not have hurt too bad.

Right leg, just under my knee. About two inches long. Straight, like it was done with a scalpel. I was around eight years old. I was tobogganing, early in the winter, and there wasn't really enough snow yet. Patches of frozen dirt and yellow grass showed where our sleds had rubbed the snow away. I was kneeling on my blue plastic crazy carpet and sliding down the hill and I leaned too much to the right, and almost rolled right off my sled. My knee scraped along the snow, and there must have been a piece of broken glass buried there or something. It sliced right through my snow pants, my jeans, my long johns, and into my leg. I don't remember how many stitches, which is weird, because we used to brag about stitches. "I needed four stitches right in my head." "Oh yeah, my brother had twenty-one when he nearly chopped his thumb off on the band saw." But I don't remember how many stitches. Maybe they used that butterfly tape. Was it even invented in 1977?

Middle finger on my right hand. Right underneath the fingernail on the left side. Shaped like a drunk comma. Slammed my finger in the passenger side door of Hector Lang's little moss green Toyota pick-up truck after Heckie took Sara and I to the Dairy Queen for Mr. Misties. Hector's dog Scotty barked non-stop until I quit crying. No stitches, but I had to wear a splint in case it was sprained.

Top of my right foot. Between my big toe and the long toe. Red and round, about the size of a watch battery. We were chasing each other around playing acorn wars and I jumped off of the Marchewa's shed on to their woodpile and landed on a piece of two-by-four with a rusty nail sticking out of it. Had to go to the hospital with the board and nail still dangling from my sticky and bloody sneaker. No stitches, but a tetanus shot.

Base of my thumb on my right hand. My sister and I got into a fight in the kitchen when my parents were both at work and she hucked a cereal bowl at me and I raised my hand to stop it and it smashed and cut my thumb pretty bad. I was about fourteen, and she was twelve. We were afraid of getting in trouble for throwing dishes at each other inside the house so we swept up every piece of broken bowl and wrapped it in a brown paper bag and took it out and snuck the evidence into the Marchewa's garbage can next door so our mom wouldn't find it. I probably needed stitches but bandaged it up and it eventually healed up without them. The scar is about an inch long, and one time when I was working on a movie set someone noticed it and told me I could never be a hand model because of it. Up until that point I didn't know being a hand model was even a real thing. Apparently you can make pretty good money being a hand model, but I am out of the running because of my scar and also because my hands don't look feminine enough to sell dish soap or jewelry and they aren't hairy or muscly enough to sell power tools or razors. The hand modeling business is pretty gendered. I looked it up after someone told me I wasn't right for it.

Two semi circles, one on either side of my chest, where my breasts used to be. About seven or eight inches long on each side. Also two small round red scars under my arms from where they put the drains in. I was forty-four years old. My first real surgery, because stitches and having an ingrown toenail removed don't count.

Two and a half years later, there is still a spot next to my sternum, just to the right of the centre of my chest where if you poke it, I feel it about four inches over, almost under my arm. Something about rearranging the nerve endings. I healed up pretty good, I think; the scars are smooth and not raised. When I am shirtless at the beach I tell myself you can't really see them, unless you are looking. They have faded, red to pink to white now, and I am very pale.

The surgeon told me in the initial consultation months before surgery that my nipples would be insensate after the operation. That I wouldn't be able to feel them at all. I heard him say the words but I told myself that the doctors have to say stuff like that, to protect themselves from lawsuits and accusations of malpractice. I told myself that doctors always give you the worst-case scenario, you know, so that you are grateful when some of the sensation comes back, so that you feel like one of the lucky ones, because you didn't have any expectations.

I didn't get to see my nipples until nearly two weeks after surgery. I had gauze bandages stitched right onto my chest to hold them in place so they could reattach to my body. I remember standing in the steaming bathroom after the first shower I had been able to have in ten days, staring down at my new shape. I have always had a little red mark on my right nipple, and found myself strangely relieved that that little red mark was still there, still on my right nipple.

I had spent an inordinate amount of time laying around healing and wondering if they had switched my nipples around when they detached them and cut them to make them smaller and then stitched them back onto me. I figured I had a fifty-fifty chance that they got it right, but had often wished in the last ten days that I had thought to remind the surgeon not to mix them up. I'm not sure why this would have bothered me, but it would have. Right one in the right spot, I thought, and smiled.

It's weird, seeing a part of your body but not being able to feel it. I've had a couple of alarming moments since surgery, one time dragging myself out of a lake onto a wooden dock, and another time when I pulled a very heavy Rubbermaid tub off of a shelf, when I scraped my chest really hard and had a heart-pounding moment, pulling my shirt up in a panic to make sure I hadn't peeled one or both of my new nipples off of myself and just couldn't feel it.

My nipples used to be so sensitive. I was one of those people who everyone always made "is it cold in here?" jokes about. My nipples were a big erogenous zone, and they brought me a lot of pleasure and heat. I loved my nipples, I just hated having breasts.

If I had had an extra thirty thousand US I would have gone to see this surgeon in New York state that I had heard about, he has developed a procedure where he keeps the nerve stem attached to the nipple intact, and can perform the mastectomy without losing nipple sensation, but I didn't have the money. So I made a deal. I traded the nipples I loved for the chest I needed. For the most part I'm happy in my new shape, and twenty-three hours and fifty-six minutes out of the day it seems worth it.

But sometimes, in the dark when she puts her palms flat on my chest and presses, or when we are on our way out to a show and she fixes my tie and smooths it down over top of my dress shirt with the red tips of her fingernails, I wish. I wish. I wish I could feel everything. The skin of my chest now seems hypersensitive, like it is trying to make up for the fact that my nipples are basically two big scars now.

They are beyond numb. They feel nothing. Sometimes I think I can feel the flesh underneath them, maybe I can feel pressure there, maybe. But I can't feel her fingertips or her tongue, or her teeth. I can't feel the cold lake or the warm sun either.

But even still, every morning that I get up and just slip a t-shirt over my head and pull my jeans on and take the little dog out, every time I swim or shower or sweat or lift weights or button up my shirt and step in front of a mirror, I feel grateful. I feel like I am standing inside the right shape of me now and I know I would make the same trade over again tomorrow if I had to.

Now, when I run, or swim, or dance, or fuck, or ride my bike really hard, I can look down, and see my own heart pounding there, just beneath the thin and tender skin of my new chest. My own heart pounding perfect, right beside my left nipple, which is exactly where it should be.

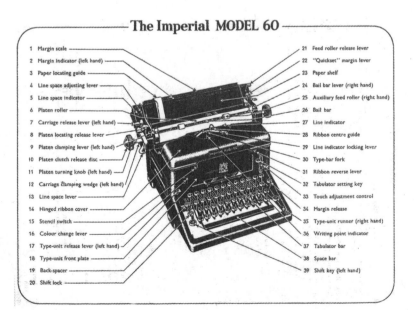

## The Imperial MODEL 60

1  Margin scale
2  Margin indicator (left hand)
3  Paper locating guide
4  Line space adjusting lever
5  Line space indicator
6  Platen roller
7  Carriage release lever (left hand)
8  Platen locating release lever
9  Platen clamping lever (left hand)
10  Platen clutch release disc
11  Platen turning knob (left hand)
12  Carriage clamping wedge (left hand)
13  Line space lever
14  Hinged ribbon cover
15  Stencil switch
16  Colour change lever
17  Type-unit release lever (left hand)
18  Type-unit front plate
19  Back-spacer
20  Shift lock

21  Feed roller release lever
22  "Quickset" margin lever
23  Paper shelf
24  Bail bar lever (right hand)
25  Auxiliary feed roller (right hand)
26  Bail bar
27  Line indicator
28  Ribbon centre guide
29  Line indicator locking lever
30  Type-bar fork
31  Ribbon reverse lever
32  Tabulator setting key
33  Touch adjustment control
34  Margin release
35  Type-unit runner (right hand)
36  Writing point indicator
37  Tabulator bar
38  Space bar
39  Shift key (left hand)

I am not saying that all femmes must love a butch, or that all butches are really or will one day be trans, or that a butch cannot love another butch in that way, please, hear me when I tell you I am not saying any of those ridiculous things.

Sometimes I imagine what if penis enlargement spam was really ads for men to become better people? More spiritually evolved? Better fathers?

Gain more for less with our patented male enhancement cream.

Would you rather have more than enough to get the job done or fall short? It's up to you.

We show you how to grow.

We give you the keys to the world of real manhood.

# STEVE SAID
# IT WOULD BE OKAY

Last fall I had a gig in Nelson, a beautiful little town tucked into the Kootenay mountains, right next to a sparkling lake. I had a day off after my show before I flew home, and everyone told me I had to visit the hot springs.

Hot springs in a cave, they said, you gotta go check it out.

"What is the change room situation like there?" I asked, and got a couple of cocked heads and raised eyebrows.

"You know, for trans people," I explained.

"Oh, that. Right." A shrug. "I'm sure it will be fine."

I went to the tourist info place at the bottom of a steep hill to get a map and some more info. The woman working behind the counter had been at my show the night before, said she loved it. I was relieved, because I figured that might mean maybe she would be a little more helpful or understanding about my next question. It's one of the privileges of being an artist, and I am not above using it when I need it.

"Is there a family change room, or a gender-neutral bathroom there, anywhere I might be able to get changed? A large tree next to the parking lot?"

Gyms and change rooms are hard places for me. Pools are harder. Tourists don't help. They are entitled, and often white and straight and from America. Used to getting what they want. Used to their comfort zone.

"You know, that is a very good question. I've never even thought about that before." I looked at her long brown braid, her manicured hands, her amethyst necklace and her open, friendly face. "How about I call ahead and just warn them you are coming? I also have a coupon here for a free admission somewhere. Let me dig it up."

She disappeared into the back office for a minute before I could protest, and I could see her pick up the phone and make a short call while she fished around in a filing cabinet. She saw me watching her through the window in the office and wiggled her fingers at me, smiled reassuringly. Came back out to the counter bringing a waft of perfume with her. Something woodsy. Amber, maybe?

"Here's your free coupon, and a map. I called my friend to tell him you are on your way. It'll be fine. Just talk to Steve at the front desk. And thanks for the show. My stomach was sore from laughing this morning. Just what I needed."

I thanked her and left. It was about an hour-long winding drive along the shoreline of the lake, and a perfect early fall day for it. I cranked up the stereo and rolled the windows down, stuck my left hand out to surf the passing wind. I could smell sun and cedar trees and dust. All the way there, I wondered just what she had said to Steve on the phone, and what Steve had said to her.

The parking lot was nearly full, which I wasn't expecting, because it was the middle of September. Used to be that most of the tourists were off the roads by then, at least up North, but I guess some folks live in those big fancy RVs year round now.

There was a t-shirt and bathing suits and sandal shop, and a tired looking guy working the front desk. On either side of the desk were two arched doorways, one with MEN'S painted in hand drawn letters over the arch, the other WOMEN'S. On the wall beside the entrance to the women's change room was a giant sign that listed all the rules. No cutoffs. No t-shirts. No running, spitting, roughhousing, no alcohol. No outside shoes.

I stepped up to the desk and the guy looked me over. "You must be the Coyote," he said. I couldn't tell if he thought this was a good or a bad thing.

"You must be Steve. You don't have a family change room here, huh?" I asked.

"Nope. But I just talked to Carol at the Chamber of Commerce. She warned me you were coming. You can just use the ladies. It'll be fine." He handed me a large thick plastic bag for my belongings.

Again I wondered just what Carol at the tourist info place had said on the phone to Steve, but I didn't ask.

"I have proper swimming trunks, but only a t-shirt for a top," I explained, pointing my thumb over my shoulder to the list of house rules.

"It'll be fine," Steve reassured me with a shrug. "Enjoy."

It wasn't that fine, but I'm used to it. There were four ladies in the change room, all in their sixties or seventies, as I expected, chatting amicably together until I rounded the corner. They all fell silent and stared at me as I smiled not too wide and not too little and headed for a private stall. I stripped quickly and stuffed my clothes into the plastic bag. Shrugged into my men's trunks and a plain black t-shirt.

There was a damp narrow tiled hallway that led out of the change room and I padded barefoot down it, not looking back. The women resumed talking as soon as I was out of sight.

Right next to the door that led outside to the poolside was another desk, with a different guy behind it. He snapped his gum and reached across the desk for my bag of belongings. There were no lockers in the change room, that wasn't the system. This guy took your bag of stuff and traded it for a numbered plastic fob on a giant brass safety pin, and put your bag of stuff in the cubbyhole in the wall behind him that matched the number on your fob.

He shook his shorn head at me. "No cotton t-shirts allowed. Says so right on the sign in the lobby. Proper swimwear only. Take it off and put it in your bag."

"Steve said it would be okay," I explained.

"Steve is wrong. And Steve just went for lunch."

"I have ... surgery scars on my chest," I said, a ball of discomfort beginning to swell in my chest and throat. "I would rather not go shirtless in the pool."

"Well you can't wear that shirt, sir."

I had just stepped out of the hallway that led out of the women's change room, and the entrance to the men's change room was ten or twelve feet away on the other side of the counter behind him, so I have no idea why he referred to me as sir, but over the years I have grown so used to the gender confusion and panic of others that I have long since ceased to expect any logic to enter these exchanges, so I didn't say anything. I just took my shirt off and handed it to him to put into my bag of stuff, which was sitting on the counter between us.

His eyes widened and rested on my bare chest. I had had top surgery about three months before, and my scars were still pretty pink and fresh looking.

"Oh. I ... I ... we can lend you a shirt. It just can't be cotton. The fibers gum up the pumps." He turned and faced the wall of cubbyholes beside him. There were two cardboard boxes on the shelf, one that had MEN'S SHIRTS written on it in black felt pen, and the other WOMEN'S SHIRTS. He turned to look at me one more time, visibly uncomfortable, and then reached up and dragged down the box of women's shirts.

By this time the ball of discomfort in me had turned to humiliation, and I was willing my eyes not to well up with tears. I nearly grabbed my bag of stuff and bolted. *Hot springs in a cave*, I repeated silently to myself and took a deep breath.

The only shirt in the box that wasn't pink or pastel yellow was a turquoise, cap-sleeved (my ex taught me what that means) nylon LuLulemon yoga shirt about three sizes too small for me. I squeezed it over my tattooed shoulders and tried in vain to pull it down far enough to cover the patch of hair that trailed from my belly button down into the waistband of my swimming shorts.

The dude swallowed awkwardly and handed me my plastic number on a safety pin. I gritted my teeth and stepped outside into the chilly, steaming poolside. Tried to ignore the stares. I was pretty much the only person there by themselves, most patrons being elderly white heterosexual couples, or foursomes of Texans, the ladies in conservative one piece swimsuits and the men in sagging trunks and faded Marine Corps tattoos. Nobody made eye contact or spoke to me. I could tell they were all wondering why the young single fella wasn't at work in the middle of a weekday, and why he was sausaged into a ladies yoga top three sizes too small for him, but nobody asked.

The shine still hasn't worn off of the feeling of swimming since my top surgery. I think my body remembers swimming when I was a kid, that skin feeling of lake and river slipping over and down my still flat chest, the wood and dirt smell of weather bleached boards on the dock warm from the sun underneath me, the unexamined freedom of being in my younger body before it changed and grew and swelled to become something else. I think water reminds me of that now, and each and every time I submerge myself it immediately becomes worth it. Floating. Breathing. The change rooms and the stares and the stupid turquoise yoga shirt became smaller in my heart somehow, and there was only me, in my only body, and that nearly too hot water soaking the road out of my bones.

The caves were pretty cool, and dark enough that I got to feel anonymous in there. I do admit that at one point in my visit I lowered myself slowly into the cold pool and pissed long and luxuriously, while making unbroken eye contact with a particularly judgmental lady with diamond rings on nearly every finger on both of her hands. I wasn't about to brave the ladies' room again unnecessarily to use the toilet. Besides, I figured, the management was kind of asking for it.

Last week at a school gig, a grade eleven kid waited a long time to talk to me after. She waited until it was just her and me left. She told me her favourite class was drama, because she got to maybe be someone else. Told me one time she got to play a man in a play because she was the tallest. Told me she only had one friend. I told her one good friend is a gift. I told her school was almost over. I told her the kids who called her names were missing out because she was awesome.

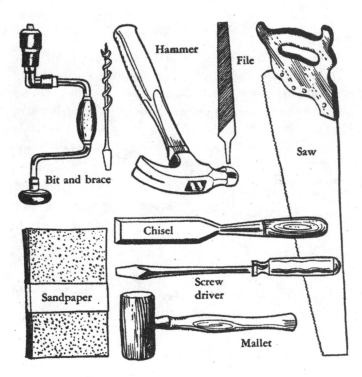

Bit and brace

Hammer

File

Saw

Chisel

Sandpaper

Screw driver

Mallet

# I WISH MY SON

This spring I got another letter. This one read:

Dear Ivan:

I just read your book *Gender Failure*. It led me to find you on YouTube and watch a few of your stories as well as interviews. A stalking of sorts.

I am a mom to four sons. That's the first time that I've said that. It's usually "a mom to three boys and a girl." This still feels strange.

My third child was born female and a little over a year ago we were told that she was a lesbian. We were shocked but supportive. She ran away about a year ago for two weeks ... and again in April and wouldn't return home until July.

Without dragging this on too long ... let's just say it was about six months of sheer hell. This is NOT normal for ANYONE in our family or extended family to run away. I was terrified, heartbroken, confused, etc.

In July we learned that he identified as a boy and soon he was calling himself Cameron.

Finally! An answer to the rebellion. I won't say it was easy, but my husband and I and his brothers have all been very supportive. I have gotten myself educated on as much as possible. I'm actually a bit embarrassed at how many online forums and meetings and books that I have read etc. I have read all of your books.

But my son is worse than ever.

He isn't happy. His pot use has escalated. He is disrespectful, hard, cold, negative. He has lost all drive and passion for anything.

He has a girlfriend and seems happy with her, but he is just so incredibly awful to me.

He sees a therapist on a regular basis. He starts testosterone on the 23rd. He says that I am the one with the problem.

I guess I'm just wondering. You have your "stuff" together. You have supportive parents. Did you ever hate your family for no reason at all?

I want so desperately for my son to have the confidence I see in you.

I want him to be happy and kind and respectful.

I don't recognize him. I was told that gender "dysphoria" is when your body doesn't match your brain. Well doesn't that mean that my kind loving thoughtful child should still be there? I feel like he died.

Any insight is appreciated.

Thanks for what you do.

I get these letters. I get these letters I can't possibly write enough or ever be wise enough to answer properly. I get these letters from good people with real questions and they turn to me with their hope and their hurts and their wondering and their whys and once I have read them they haunt me like ghosts, ghosts that follow me and whisper into my ear when I think I'm alone in the elevator. They walk half a step behind me on the sidewalk as I totter around the block with my old, deaf, and blind dog and ask me over and over just what I am I going to say to that?

I am sorry it has been months and I am just writing you back now. I am writing you back but I have to say this right at the start: I don't have anything figured out all the way. Just today I scared a woman again enough for her to scream at me in the women's change room at the gym, and you would think I would be so used to this by now that it wouldn't bother me anymore, but I cried alone in my truck in the underground parking after because I have been working out at that same gym now for twenty-three years and everyone knows me by name except the new folks like her, but still she felt like she belonged in there more than I ever will. She felt like she belonged in there enough to decide that I didn't belong. And I know what you are thinking, but I can't use the men's change room because I have been working out there for twenty-three years and what would all the old ex boxers with their bleeding tattoos and their silver chest hair have to say if I all of a sudden started peeling my jeans off next to them in their change room? Public bathrooms and change rooms for me have always been a choice between very uncomfortable and potentially unsafe, so I try to be polite about it because if I get angry it becomes so much easier for them to dismiss me, plus, an angry someone who looks like a man in the ladies' change room? Then I am seen as even more of a threat. Then it's even more all my fault.

Most days I bend and stretch inside the bit of space I have made for myself in this world, and breathe a little deeper in the spaces trans people are fighting to make bigger. Most days I can see the changes happening. Most days. Then there are other days when I cry in the truck on my own because it happened again and I'm tired of talking about it, tired of talking to anyone.

But some days the world piles up behind my eyes and on my shoulders and the fear gets in. I had a panic attack about it in the shower this morning. I haven't even told my closest friends. I'm only writing this to you now because the ghosts in my ears demand that I write you only the truth, because the truth is all that I have to give you.

It's true, my mother is very supportive. The other day we were talking on the phone and she told me about a recent trip she and her partner had taken to Skagway, Alaska.

"Remember that little fish shop that used to be right down on the wharf in the marina?" she asked me. "Well, it burned down so they rebuilt it, and when I went in there to use the washroom, they had two bathrooms, and instead of men's or women's, the signs on both doors read EITHER/OR. So, they nearly got it, but not quite, right? I mean, they were not gendered bathrooms, so that is a definite improvement, but either and or kind of still supports the claim that there are only two genders and every body has to fit into one, right? But at least you could be safe in there. I'd love for us to go back to Skagway again together sometime. You loved it so much when you were little. All those waterfalls and artists."

It's hard to describe the love I felt for my sixty-six-year-old, born-and-raised-and-still-living-in-the-Yukon Catholic mother at that moment, that kind of love that threatens to tear a hole out of your eyes or your chest or your heart because it just got so big so fast and there nearly wasn't enough room inside me to hold all of it.

I could tell you that there were a lot of long hard years between that conversation and the one I had with her when I was eighteen years old and just coming out of the closet. I could tell you that I found it easier to write the words "I am trans" down on paper and publish them in a book that perfect strangers could pick up and read than it was for me to come right out and speak those words out loud to most of my family. I could tell you that there are things about me that my mother learned from reading my books that I still don't have the ovaries to say right to her face, to this day.

I could tell you that my father, most of my uncles, and one of my aunts refuse to call me by anything but my birth name, even though I have been going by Ivan now for longer than I used the name I was born with. Even though it says Ivan in my passport, even though I lose a little bit of my heart every time anyone I love calls me by my old name, even though I wouldn't think to turn around anymore if I heard it called out on the street. Some trans activists call this my "deadname." I feel uncomfortable with this term but I still haven't figured out why.

How old is your son? You didn't say for sure in your letter, or in the short response to my quick email I first wrote you telling you I was going to need some time to answer you. My guess is around seventeen? I wonder if it would be of any comfort for you to time travel with me back to 1987 in Whitehorse, Yukon? I wonder how confident I would seem to you in grade twelve? I hadn't even come out of the closet as queer, and I wouldn't dare to even whisper the word trans in the mirror for nearly two more decades.

I see my friends from high school still, mostly on Facebook, we are all pushing fifty now, somehow, and have all learned the hard hard lesson that the things that gave us swagger and got us laid in grade eleven don't amount to much bank when it comes to getting a promotion at work or paying for your kids' braces or helping your aunt kick breast cancer.

All this to say that I wouldn't put too much stock in your son's confidence levels just yet. He is learning to be a man in a way that probably none of the men he has ever met will be able to help him with. His own father, father of three other sons, doesn't know yet how to help this son.

Except to love him, which it sounds like his father does. This is a gift.

I don't hate my father. I just know there are places in me, things about me, that he will never understand, that he doesn't want to understand. I try not to let this hurt anything but the surface of me, but it pushes a space between us, a little wider every time I hang up the phone or wave goodbye. He never asks me how I am, what I am doing, who I love or who loves me, so every day that passes I become more of a stranger to him, I guess. I have learned to make this our normal, and try to concentrate on the things we have in common, the interests we share, but I don't get out boating or fishing too much these days, so mostly I just listen.

My cousin Dianne's son is about to graduate from high school. His name is Liam, and he is seventeen, a huge strapping kid just like his father, who I knew back in high school. He read *Gender Failure* and did a report on it for his English class. He wrote me an email to ask me some questions for his project. My favourite part of his letter was:

"My research paper, aimed mainly at the general public who have never even thought about how gender isn't black and white, attempts to explore thoughts on being trans and how it differs from and should not be categorized as a disorder. I recently read your book *Gender Failure* and it gave me the inspiration for my research paper. I was hoping you would be able to give me some more insight on the topic and maybe answer a few questions. I can prepare questions and email you, or if you would prefer you can come up with questions you think would be most beneficial for my research."

I haven't seen this second cousin of mine since he was about thirteen, I think, but he knows more about parts of me than my own father does, and he learned them from reading a book my father will most likely never pick up.

My family is huge. My family is complicated. I have loved and hated nearly all of them for both good and selfish reasons at some point in my life. I consider myself one of the very lucky ones, my scales always tip towards loving most of them nearly all of the time. I forgive them their trespasses and imperfections and hope that they love me enough to do likewise. It took me over forty years to accept myself. I didn't fully come to terms with being and calling myself trans until a couple of years ago. So, by that math, I give them another forty-two years of practice before I will start to expect them all to have it down perfect. Fair is fair.

If I were to meet your son, and he were to ask my advice, which is unlikely, I would tell him this:

If you are going to be a man, then please, be a good man. Be a kind man. Be a feminist man. Do not try to fit into mainstream male culture by rejecting and reviling the feminine, not in you, not in others, and not in the world.

This is the same advice I would give all seventeen-year-old men, the only difference being that I will expect more from your son, I cannot help myself. I have been proven wrong on this on multiple occasions, but still, I will continue to expect more from him than I do cisgender boys his age. He already knows that much of what he has been taught about being a woman or a man is not true for him, so it must not be true for others, too. I will expect him to know and remember this.

I would tell him that the more that I am read as male, the more important it is for me to be conscious of the way I move through the world. I don't tell women on the street they look beautiful today, even when they really do. I make sure I don't walk too closely behind them in the park or on the street after dark. I keep my hands and feet and knees and gaze to myself on public transit. I remember that what reads as impatience or frustration from a woman waiting in a bank line-up can feel like anger or aggression coming from a man.

I would tell him to cry in public as much as he wants, just to make more room for everyone to cry. I would tell him I am crying as I write this right now.

I would tell him to write poems instead of punching walls.

I would tell him that being trans is hard, but no matter how difficult it is, all that pain and frustration is never to be used as an excuse to mistreat the people closest to you. I would tell him that this is like screaming at a driver who cut you off on the freeway with all the windows rolled up in both vehicles: the bad driver doesn't hear you, in fact, he is already ten cars ahead of you, probably oblivious. The only person who can hear you is your girlfriend sitting beside you, or your grandmother, or your son or daughter.

I would tell him to try to be kinder to his mother, that she is doing the best she can to understand.

I never really related to the theory that being trans meant my body didn't match my brain. I feel like this is a handy narrative that puts all of the pressure and responsibility for change onto trans people and off of the rest of society. If we could just grow a beard or not have a penis or an Adam's apple, if we were shorter or taller or skinnier or hairier or less hairy, if our breasts were bigger or removed, if we could take and somehow pay for and heal from all the steps we would need to go through so that nobody could tell anymore that we were trans, then we could be happy. I did have top surgery nearly four years ago, after binding my breasts down for nineteen years, and that was the right thing for me. It was the healthy, happy thing for me to do, and I will always be grateful that I live in a country and province where this was covered under my medical plan. Not because the government decided this was the right thing, but because many trans people fought for years to make it so. Trans people should absolutely have access to required surgeries and hormone treatment as wanted or necessary. To me, that is a given.

But my day-to-day struggles are not so much between me and my body. I am not trapped in the wrong body; I am trapped in a world that makes very little space for bodies like mine. I live in a world where public washrooms are a battle ground, where politicians can stand up and be applauded for putting forth an amendment barring me from choosing which gendered bathroom I belong in. I live in a world where my trans sisters are routinely murdered without consequence or justice. I live in a world where trans youth get kicked out onto the street by their parents who think their God is standing behind them as they close their front doors on their own children. Going to the beach is an act of bravery for me. None of this is a battle between me and my own flesh. For me to be free, it is the world that has to change, not trans people.

I know that your kind and loving and thoughtful child is still there. I know he needs you to love him right now, to help make up for a world that often does not.

And how about you? What kind of support or community do you have around you? I hope it consists of more than a letter from a storyteller that took three months to arrive. Please reach out to find other parents of trans kids. I am sure you will find some comfort and recognition there.

There is no one right, monolithic trans narrative, and the more trans youth you meet, the more you will see what I see: that trans youth are resilient and beautiful, and inventive and brave and hilarious, and that many of them are happy.

My aunt Nora told me a few years ago that all through my teens she could see that I wasn't comfortable in my own skin, but that she had no words for what seemed to be troubling me, and so had no way to help me.

It is thirty years later, and we have words for what is troubling your son, and he has found them and is using them, and so are you, and so are his father and brothers. He has a mother who loves him enough to write someone and ask for help. He is already thirty years ahead of me.

I think that is pretty much all the advice this childless writer dares give you. Please give my best to your son and the rest of your family, and please, keep in touch.

Today in the heart-rending world of small-town school shows, I met another trans kid. Grade nine. Struggling. Unstable housing, mother with addiction issues, other kids not respecting his chosen name and pronoun. He says he's getting a job so he can buy a binder because he can't handle looking at them. He tells me the first time he told his mom he was trans she was blacked out and didn't remember the mean things she said to him. But he remembered. He told me that before his people were colonized, two-spirit people were respected, did I know that? We hugged. I told him I would send him some books when I got home, care of the school. He said he had four good friends that he could trust. I said now you have five. He said I know. I told him keep on drawing, that art will help you get through. He said I know.

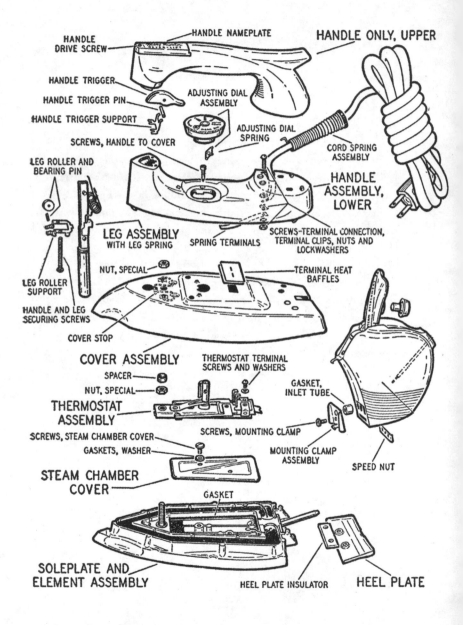

HANDLE DRIVE SCREW

HANDLE NAMEPLATE

HANDLE ONLY, UPPER

HANDLE TRIGGER

HANDLE TRIGGER PIN

HANDLE TRIGGER SUPPORT

ADJUSTING DIAL ASSEMBLY

ADJUSTING DIAL SPRING

CORD SPRING ASSEMBLY

SCREWS, HANDLE TO COVER

LEG ROLLER AND BEARING PIN

HANDLE ASSEMBLY, LOWER

LEG ASSEMBLY WITH LEG SPRING

NUT, SPECIAL

SPRING TERMINALS

SCREWS-TERMINAL CONNECTION, TERMINAL CLIPS, NUTS AND LOCKWASHERS

LEG ROLLER SUPPORT

HANDLE AND LEG SECURING SCREWS

TERMINAL HEAT BAFFLES

COVER STOP

COVER ASSEMBLY

THERMOSTAT TERMINAL SCREWS AND WASHERS

SPACER

NUT, SPECIAL

GASKET, INLET TUBE

THERMOSTAT ASSEMBLY

SCREWS, STEAM CHAMBER COVER

GASKETS, WASHER

SCREWS, MOUNTING CLAMP

MOUNTING CLAMP ASSEMBLY

SPEED NUT

STEAM CHAMBER COVER

GASKET

SOLEPLATE AND ELEMENT ASSEMBLY

HEEL PLATE INSULATOR

HEEL PLATE

# WE'VE GOT A SITUATION HERE

After about fifteen years of doing my anti-bullying show in Canadian public schools, I finally got invited to bring the show into a few high schools in the US. In Eugene, Oregon. I had been to the University of Oregon the previous spring, and had done a gig for a group of teacher candidates at the university, and I think one of those fresh-out-of-the-wrapper young teachers contacted my agent that books all my school gigs, and they put a little high school tour together.

That same young teacher had originally seen me do a public show for adults in the evening. A show where maybe I swore a little bit and talked about top surgery and queer politics. This well-intentioned young teacher for some reason thought maybe I would trot out some of that same material for her ninth graders at a public school in smallish-town Oregon. The reality is that the show I take into public high schools is pretty tame. I tell a couple of stories, one about the summer that me, my little sister, and my cousins Dan and Christopher spent living with my grandmother in Nanaimo, BC. We were living on the very fixed income of a retired and frugal woman, and one day she bought us all used roller-skates at the Salvation Army Thrift Store. My clumsy and often bullied cousin Christopher wiped out in the first ten minutes of the first day we had those roller skates and pooped his shorts. This story is designed to engage and entertain up to 1,000 kids aged eleven to seventeen and attempt to keep them from texting each other or falling asleep for approximately fifty-five minutes. I'm also attempting to get them to sympathize, empathize, or at least feel sorry for or protective of my poor little cousin.

I tell another story right after the roller-skating one about being mistaken for a young man on an airplane by forty fifteen-year-old volleyball players on their way to a tournament. This story flashes back to my own high school experience with mean girls, and how I still carry the marks on my heart to this day.

Then we do a brief question-and-answer period. Sometimes it takes four or five questions about how did I get into writing and how many tattoos do I have, and what kind of music do I like, but almost every single time a usually young and scrawny for his age boy puts up his hand and asks me where my cousin Christopher is now?

This is when I take a deep breath and tell the kids that my cousin committed suicide in his very early twenties, and then we have an often very moving discussion about high-school bullying and its consequences.

I've toured this show in small-town schools all over the country, and done it in front of kids as young as grade four, in Catholic schools in Newfoundland, in the bible belt of the Fraser Valley, in both the junior and senior high schools in Whitehorse that I graduated from. I've received thank you letters and emails from marginalized kids, bullies, former bullies, future bullies, teachers, counsellors, principals, and even a used-to-be bullied kid who now works as a janitor in an inner-city school in Toronto.

I don't say the word queer or trans unless it comes up in a question from one of the students. There is no sexual content in the show whatsoever. The moral of the whole show is basically to be kind to your fellow students. In fifteen years I have never received even a single complaint about any of the show's content, and I've taken it into some very small blue-collar towns in some pretty remote parts of the country.

But for some reason this young teacher was worried I would trot out some of the stuff she had seen me do at my university reading the previous spring, and so decided it would be a great idea to send one of those consent letters out to the parents of 700 kids, asking permission for their child to attend my presentation about gay issues, and she included links to my website.

This of course alarmed those parents who were already prone to alarm, and they immediately forwarded the email to the easily alarmable parents in the other schools I was booked to perform in. A group of self-described "concerned parents" then proceeded to scour the internet for the least appropriate YouTube clips of me performing at cabarets in nightclubs at one a.m., and then sent a rash of hysterical emails to each other about all the horribly queer things I was about to say in front of their ninth-grade kids in a public school next week.

The school board was contacted. Stern letters were composed. The superintendent of the entire school district was alerted. Several parents refused to allow their kids to attend my presentation, and the concerned parents group decided that they were going to attend and disrupt my presentation at the first sign of problematic content. The kids from the Gay/Straight Alliance at the school caught wind of the trouble brewing and became outraged at the injustice of it all. They invited the GSA kids from neighbouring schools to come to my gig and stand in solidarity with them in support of me. They used money they had raised from a fundraiser and had shirts made up with a picture of me on it, complete with an inspiring quote from my young adult book, and broke out all of their rainbow regalia.

I was not notified about any of this controversy at all. The school counsellor just sent me an email a few days before clarifying that there was no foul language in my presentation, which I assured her there was not.

It was raining that late January morning. My first clue that something was up was the group of rainbow-clad kids shivering under shared umbrellas outside the front doors of their school. There was even a giant rainbow flag borne by a long-eyelashed pretty boy with half of his hair shaved off and the other half dyed crimson and turquoise. He had borrowed one of those belts that hold the base of a flagpole and strapped it around his slender waist and shoved the giant flagpole into it. He weighed about eighty-five pounds soaking wet, which he was, and every time the wind picked up he was forced to take several wobbly dance-like steps in a row, first one way, and then the other, to avoid being tipped over or blown away altogether by the gusts catching the rainbow flag he valiantly clung onto, which was in danger of being turned into a giant gay mainsail.

The kids cheered as I stepped out of my truck. This had never happened to me before, and I felt my cheeks flush and my ears burn red.

This is right about when the concerned parents began to arrive. In a long train of black SUVs. These parents were so concerned by what I was about to say to their fourteen-year-olds that they had brought their toddlers with them too, and as each SUV pulled up and opened its doors, clusters of blonde women with long dresses that covered their wrists, ankles, and necks got out of the black vehicles, clutching their toddlers while their husbands unfolded strollers and opened umbrellas.

The principal met me just inside the glass doors and ushered me into her office and shut the door. She looked nervous and was clutching a walkie-talkie.

"We've got a situation here," she informed me, her mouth written in a grim line in the middle of her strong jawline. She was wearing Fleuvogs and a chocolate brown leather pencil skirt, which for some reason I took as sign that everything was going to be okay.

The principal told me what was going on with the concerned parents and the superintendent and the school board and the angry queer kids and the nervous counsellors and the extra security she had to hire and the walkie-talkies, and then told me not to worry about any of it and just go ahead and do my show like nothing was going on. She said this like she actually thought this was possible.

I asked her for directions to the staff washroom, and locked the door behind me. I peed, splashed some water on my face, drank a little tap water, buttoned up the top button of my denim shirt, unbuttoned it, then buttoned it back up again. I straightened the pocket square in the left pocket of my jacket, and told my reflection to just go out there and do what I do. Told myself to be brave, just like the tattoo on the inside of my left wrist said to be.

The concerned parents were all lined up along the right side of the gym next to the double doors that led out into the hallway. About thirty of them, mostly women, almost all blonde, nearly all of them with small even blonder children squirming in their laps.

The superintendent of the school district approached me and shook my hand, introduced himself and a couple of his colleagues. We all just acted like this was a normal day at the office. Like there was not a row of blonde evangelicals lined up waiting for something, anything to happen that they could find fault with.

The kids were filing in, about 500 of them, from the seventh to the tenth grades. The kid with the rainbow flag was now sitting in the last row of bleachers, his flagpole still raised high, but propped against the concrete wall behind him, the flag now limp and still damp. The rest of the rainbow kids had already claimed their seats in the first couple of rows of bleachers, directly in front of the solo microphone on a stand that stood just a few feet in front of the face-off circle. This meant that when I stood in front of the microphone I would be looking directly into a block of oversized black t-shirts with an image of my own face on them. The wood floor of the gym was old but well-loved and polished to a high shine.

The principal stepped up to the microphone and reminded the kids that there was a bake sale on Friday, and to please turn off their cell phones and put them away. A nervous pair of androgynous kids from the Gay/Straight Alliance stepped up in tandem and read a mumbly introduction of me not quite into the microphone, so that almost none of the other kids could hear a word of what either of them was saying.

I stepped up to the microphone amidst a smattering of vaguely confused and half-hearted applause.

I took a deep breath and reached right down into the bottom of me and did the very best show I could muster up. I gave those kids 200 percent that morning, and a couple of minutes in I had them laughing and leaning forward to listen. I didn't even look sideways at the moral majority seated sternly in their folding chairs, I kept my eyes locked on the kids who looked like they were having most of the fun and pretended it was just us in the gymnasium together. They had a good time, and five minutes in I felt my adrenaline cease circling around in my chest and begin to flow down my arms and legs, and I used every bit of it to inhabit those stories and tell the living shit out of them.

The kids had fun, I could tell.

All I had to do was make it unscathed through the question-and-answer session, and I was out of there.

Several arms shot up when I asked if they had any questions for me. One of the very first questions was where was my cousin Christopher now. I told the kid that they had a choice of two options. Option A was I would make up a happy Disney ending for him, where my clumsy awkward bullied cousin grew up to be a tall and handsome man who lived happily ever after, or I could tell them all the truth.

The truth. Tell us the truth, the kids called out, and so I did. I told them my cousin died of a self-inflicted gunshot wound to the head just before Christmas the year he should have turned twenty-three years old, and that I believed that this had happened largely because of how he had been treated by other kids all throughout his years in public school. I told them that was why I was there, to talk about school culture, and how to make schools safer for all of us. The room got quieter and the kids sat up straight, their faces sober and somber.

A slender young guy slouched on one of the middle bleachers raised his hand and held it there.

"Yes, you, right there with the Boy George t-shirt on," I said. He looked around him, like there might be other Boy George t-shirts in his vicinity, and pointed to his own chest, me?

I nodded.

He flicked his long highlighted bangs out of his eyes, which immediately returned to their place directly in front of his eyes. He paused and then spoke.

"I'm sorry about your cousin," he said.

I thanked him.

"Anyway," he continued, "I don't mean to be rude or anything, because you are a very good stand-up comedian and everything, and I had fun and all, but I had to get up like, over an hour earlier than my usual time so I could get bussed in here for this, because I go to Pine Crest Alternative school and our whole GSA came here especially to hear you perform today, and well, no offense, but you didn't say a single gay thing at all."

I felt the evangelicals lean forward in their seats, holding their collective breath. This is it, I could feel them thinking.

The principal placed her hand on the walkie-talkie clipped to the waistband of her pencil skirt.

I smiled at the kid, let my shoulders relax.

"Well," I said, "thank you for travelling to see me perform. I'm honoured, and it's great to see so many proud and out students here today. You all give me hope, you truly do. I was not as brave as you when I was fourteen. I wasn't brave enough to come out until after I graduated from high school, and I'm so very proud of you, I am. But I'm actually here for every single kid in this gym today. Every last one of you. Because I think we all deserve to be able to go to school and get a public education without fear or harassment or emotional, physical, or spiritual violence. No matter what race you are, or your gender, gender identity, or sexuality," I paused, giving a half a glance sideways to the row of concerned Christian parents. "Or your religion, no matter who you are or what you believe, or how you look or who you love, you have a right to feel safe in your school. I won't stop working until all of you do."

We talked for a bit, I can't remember about what exactly now, the adrenaline was starting to turn into tired and hungry and I felt a bit light headed. I needed another coffee, bad.

After it was over, the principal shook my hand hard and posed for a picture with a manicured hand around my shoulder for the school newspaper. The superintendent thanked me and gave me his business card. I got several hugs from sweaty ninth-grade boys with fragrant armpits and soft voices. More hugs and a huge round of selfies with the GSA kids. Some tears. Theirs at first, and then mine, too. A girl from the eighth grade who loomed a foot taller than the rest of her peers gave me a bouquet of roses she had made completely out of coat hangers and three different colours of duct tape. They smelled like fake vanilla. I asked her why and she said it was because they really smelled like duct tape so she sprayed them with the air freshener she found in the gender-neutral bathroom in the nurse's office. The bell sounded for lunch and the gym emptied as the hallways filled. I picked up my water bottle and headed out the side door of the gym, walked across the waterlogged grass to the parking lot, and found my truck.

There was a man waiting on the sidewalk. I had seen him earlier, driving one of the black SUVs full of evangelical Christian protestors. As soon as he saw me he stepped forward, holding the lapels of his suit jacket closed against the wind, placing his sturdy body between me and my vehicle. Squinting from under his red-blond eyebrows against the stinging rain.

Fuck, I thought. I can't handle a confrontation. I haven't eaten. Those free breakfast rooms in mid-range hotels depress the shit out of me, especially in the US. I should have gotten up earlier. All I had in me was a banana and a black coffee. Things were going so good. Just be cool, I told myself. You did your job. You did okay. Don't ruin it all by getting snippy when this asshole tells you you're going to burn in hell for eternity or that you are spreading disease or whatever it is that is about to come out of his mouth. I took another deep breath and stopped, my keys clinking against my stainless steel water bottle. Almost every school I perform in gives me a school water bottle, or a hoodie bearing the name of their school team. I've got one of nearly every animal. The Hawks. The Cougars (I save those and give them to my friends as jokes). The Tigers. The Bears. My favourite is the Garden City Gophers from Winnipeg. I've always had a thing for the underdogs, and the Gophers always ended up in the semi-finals with the Grizzlies from the other side of town. I will always root for the small but determined rodent in a battle with a giant fanged mammal any day, I guess it's just my nature.

Anyway. I took a deep breath and stood there, waiting for this guy to tell me what an abomination I was. A woman that I assumed was his wife and another woman and several kids were waiting in the SUV behind him, staring solemnly at me through rain-streaked windows.

He shook my hand and introduced himself. Stephen something, I didn't hear his last name and didn't ask him to repeat it.

"Might I have a word?" he asked, and I nodded, looking over his shoulder to see if the principal or any of the school board folks were still milling about. They were not.

He cleared his throat, played with the loose knot in his necktie, glanced over his shoulder at the waiting vehicle. Smiled at me.

"I wanted to tell you how moved I was by your presentation today."

I tried not to let my jaw fall open.

"Really," he continued, "and I have to be honest and tell you I did not come here today expecting to enjoy myself. Quite the contrary, in fact. We all came here because we were pretty convinced we would disagree with most of what you had to say. We intended to ... inter ... uh ... to speak up if you said something we found particularly offensive or problematic. And I can only speak for myself, but that is not what happened for me here today at all."

I let a tentative smile reach my face as he continued.

"Your cousin was twenty-two, you said, when he … passed?"

I nodded. "He was twenty-two. And a half."

His eyes began to fill with tears, making them look startlingly blue in all that grey sky.

"I was twenty-one when I first attempted suicide," he confessed, as a giant tear escaped and rolled down his stubbled cheek. He glanced over his shoulder, then looked back at me. His face looked weather-worn, like he worked outside.

"I grew up in a very small town in a very big Mormon family. I had a real tough time at school too, like your cousin. I thought I had gotten over most of it, you know, put it in the past, but today, well, listening to your stories about Christopher, it all came rushing back to me. I was expecting to be offended by what you had to say, not moved. The good Lord brought you to me to teach me, and I thank you."

I didn't know what to say. We stood there for a moment, looking right into each other's eyes.

"I'm so glad you made it through," I told him. "And here we are today. I have to tell you I did not expect your words to me to be kind ones. Maybe we both learned something."

He nodded. His chin was puckering a little, his eyes shining with tears. He blinked them back.

"Do you have a kid that goes to school here?"

He pinched the bridge of his nose between his fingertips. I do that too sometimes, when I am trying not to cry.

"My daughter, Hope. She's in the eighth grade."

"Do you think Hope is having a better time at school than you did?"

He expelled a large breath, like he had been holding it in and it hurt a little. "So far, so good, I think. She's only twelve. She and I can really talk. We're good friends."

"So many kids are not that lucky," I told him.

"Yeah," he said. "I sure wasn't."

Then he shook my hand again, shook his head to get it together, turned and jumped into the SUV and drove off, his winter tires hum-singing against the wet pavement.

His hand had felt like cracked leather. Firm grip, the kind that doesn't realize how hard it felt in my writer's hand.

I got the feeling he would have hugged me if we had been alone.

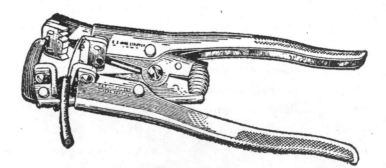

# KRAFT SINGLES
# FOR EVERYONE

My grandmother Florence Amelia Mary Daws died on May 13, 2009. She was almost ninety years old. There were twenty of us in the room, including my gran, when she passed.

Her children, my uncle Dave the Catholic priest, my uncle Laurence the furniture salesman, my aunt Nora the accountant and her husband Kevin the electrician, my aunt Roberta the telephone operator, and my mom, a retired government worker.

Her grandchildren, my cousins, Dan, Jennifer, Katy, Lindsay, Rachael, Robert, Dan's wife Sarah, Lindsay's fiancée Cameron, Robert's girlfriend Dana, and myself, the third generation of us. Florence's grandchildren are a tattoo artist, a personal assistant, her father's furniture salesman, a hospital office worker, stripper, brew master, librarian, fireman/carpenter, med student (not related by blood), and a writer/storyteller.

Dan and Sarah's daughter Layla was there too, and unbeknownst to anyone but perhaps fifteen-year-old Layla, there was a fifth-generation present that day too, a small fetus that would one day become little Odin.

Why do I list us all? Because this matters.

I just read this over, to make sure I didn't forget anyone. I did. I forgot my mom's boyfriend Chuck. Chuck's a good guy. Quiet, not like the rest of us, which is maybe why I forgot him the first go-round. And oh yeah, Jennifer and Katy's husbands Rod and Mike were both at home in Vancouver, taking care of the kids. The ones too little yet for stuff like why do we all have to die one day, Grandpa? And how did a little tiny grey lady like her make so many big giant babies like all of us? How did that happen? An even harder question to explain to little ones than where do we come from is where do we go when we are done here? At least in my family. Sex and death. Hard topics for the Catholics. Always have been. Even us recovering ones.

So. This is my family, the Daws side anyway. This is a story of ours, a big story, and like all big family stories, it is made up of many little ones, and was many years unfolding.

My mom called me on a Sunday night. I had just landed from a long spell on the road, just crawled into bed in fact when the phone rang. All she had to say was, "It's your gran. I think maybe it's time. I think you better come home."

And so I did. I flew home the next morning and arrived in the Whitehorse airport first thing, bleary-eyed and all the edges blurry. My mom and my Aunt Nora were there to meet me, they loaded my suitcase into the trunk of Nora's little car, and we drove straight to the hospital. Didn't even go home first. It was raining. I remember that it was raining.

My mom stopped me with one small cold hand on my shoulder outside the hospital room door.

"Tell me," she said. "I need you to tell me honestly, how does she look? It is hard for us to really see her anymore, she's been slipping so slowly."

I thought I had steeled myself, but still my stomach fell like a stone at the sight of my grandmother, so impossibly small now under the thin blue hospital blanket, just a slip of her left between the two rises of her grey head and gnarled old toes.

"Talk to her," my uncle said, and waved two fingers, "the nurses say she can still hear us."

And so we did. We talked. To her, to each other. Remember her bad cooking? Baloney roast? Boiled hamburger? Lemon hard cake, cousin Dan had dubbed her attempt at meringue. How she loved us all, no matter who we were, no matter what we did, her whole band of misfits. I am so proud of you, she would say. That was all she ever said. Never questioned us, except, "And have you been to mass lately? A bit of church never hurt anyone, you know."

I volunteered for night shift and sat next to the laboured-breathing shape of her with my two uncles, whispering stories through the dark to each other. Once or twice she opened one eye, staring scared at nothing. "She's not really awake," the boys said. "It's just the pain that brings her back." And the nurse would come in and give her a needle and she would disappear back into her broken hipbone coma dreams.

Just before dawn, her sons slipped downstairs to smoke. I held her hand, cold blue veins mapping her nearly ninety years, her skin now worn so soft and thin.

And then she moved. She squeezed my hand and opened both eyes, blinking, surprised that she still breathed, seemed to me. Tried to speak. Struggled with her mask. I pulled it from her mouth and leaned in close. She whispered that she loved me 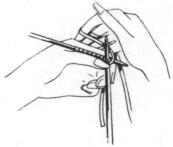 and then the boys burst back into the room.

"She's awake," I scream-whispered, and the northern spring sun made the dust bits dance in the beginning of this day.

"It's just the pain," said Dave. "I'll get the nurse." I shook my head, and dragged Laurence over.

"She is here," I repeated. "Say something, she was talking to me just now I swear it, say something she would like, go ahead and see for yourself."

Laurence leaned in and her eyes widened at the sight of him. "Mum," he said. "I'm here, and know what? I took a paid holiday to come up. I'm getting paid right now."

"Good boy," she gasped, and he stood up straight.

"It is her," he said. "Call everyone right now, she heard me all right."

My cousin Robert came in around six and she half smiled, reached for his hand a little. "Guess what, Gran," he said, "I got half price on my plane ticket home for bereavement."

"Good boy too," she squawked, and we all laughed because she was back in the room with us and she wasn't before, not like this.

She remained awake and sort of talking until everyone showed up and then the coma came again and stayed. She died the next morning, surrounded by all of us, her babies and their babies and their babies too. All of us around what was left of her in a circle with our hands touching her like it was a ritual, which was weird because we are Irish Catholic Yukoners and we don't really do rituals, unless they involve a TV show on a certain night or maybe Sunday roast with those little canned peas and also roast potatoes with the skins off.

Anyway, her tiny chest rose and fell and then stopped, and I saw it, I saw her spirit leave her, really, it was like it was her one second and then no more breath and no more her, where she had been just then was now something else just a shell maybe or something, and what is the difference I used to think but now I know because I saw it happen watched her leave herself. I hesitate to say her death was beautiful, because it means I have to miss her now, but it was.

And I don't want to sound weird here but when she left, she left something behind in me, I felt it enter through my fingers and settle itself deep inside my marrow like her blood in me but even better, immortal. And sometimes now I can feel her, she is almost right here, still in the room somewhere, she lives. Everything she gave me, I still have.

Every time I recycle a Ziploc bag, every day that I work hard, every time I remember to be grateful, she lives in me. Every time I remember my scarf and gloves, every time I eat the leftovers instead of letting them go to waste. Every time I eat a raspberry hard candy and stuff a used Kleenex into my jacket pocket. Every time I light a candle, she is there in me. Every time I have faith.

So maybe that is what it is called. My inheritance. Maybe what she left me was faith. And by faith, I do not just mean faith in God. I mean so much more than just that.

I have thought about heaven a lot, the last few years, as does everyone who mourns and wants to believe, wants to remember. Some thoughts on heaven? I have this theory that heaven is different for everyone. It has to be, or it wouldn't be heaven. My grandmother's heaven? In her heaven she doesn't have to share the remote with anyone, and it is *Jeopardy!* and *Wheel of Fortune* on all the time, with nary a rerun ever, and the old lady always wins the big money and a trip to Europe to tour a castle or somewhere warm but not too hot with nice churches. In her heaven your knees don't hurt and your back doesn't hurt and you get to be whatever age was your favourite age to be and you still have all your teeth and there are bingo games right after dinner and raspberry hard candies and no one ever has to do the dishes. In my gran's heaven, you can still have yourself a proper smoke in the living room and it doesn't ruin the new paint job and the lawn never gets too long and the foxes don't chase the birds off the birdfeeder. In her heaven, a nice bit of cheese won't give you the bad stomach and real men don't beat their wives or fuck their children, and every day is payday, and the Friday of a long weekend. Floors wax themselves, but you still get to hang the laundry, but only if you feel like it.

My wee gran has been dead now for seven years. I am seven years older and she is not. She will never be any older, only younger, and laughing, and sweeping, and having a thimbleful of brandy at the kitchen table late at night, for her throat troubles.

This last October 21 was my gran's birthday. She would have been ninety-five, but she is not. My mom and aunties went to the graveyard to put flowers and say hello and to do the rosary for her. (It's a Catholic thing, it's kind of boring except for the part where you get to say, "Fruit of thy womb, Jesus," which for some reason cracked us all up when we were little.) When I am home, I like to drive up past her house and up to Grey Mountain to the cemetery to visit her there and talk to her, even though the thought of her little bent body and tired old bones alone in all that permafrost slays me every time I have to leave her.

I know it is only her bones in that cold box. I know this. I still wish her bones didn't have to be alone. I wish we could have buried her in her own back yard, under the patch of lawn, next to the pole for the clothesline that my cousin Dan carved and painted a sunflower into, because they were her favourite, next to fireweed and cornflowers and the humble poppy because they come back every year on their own steam. The dogs would run around in circles on top of her, and the back yard would smell like the dryer vent on Saturdays, and she would be impressed at how the cucumbers did even with all the rain we got last spring and that late frost we got second week in June if you can believe that nonsense.

But it is illegal to bury someone in their own back yard, however beloved they might have been. Apparently someone misused the privilege at some point and went and ruined it all for the rest of us.

So her bones lie up at Grey Mountain cemetery in Whitehorse, up at the top of a cliff that overlooks her back yard. My grandfather, her husband, is up there too, ever since I was nine years old. We buried her way on the other side of the field from where he is. No one even suggested we put her anywhere near him. It never even came up. I will be there too, one day, if my wishes are respected by whoever is around to follow them out. I am a bit superstitious about going back into the same dirt you were born on. The graveyard is about three kilometres as the crow flies away from the hospital where my mom had me when she was nineteen. The circle of my skin and bones will end almost exactly where it started.

My cousin Dan told us all a story on the second afternoon of us sitting around in the hospital, about how last fall when Layla was showing the monster side of her teenage self and skipping out of school a lot, Dan had cooked up a deal with my gran. Since Layla just did not seem able to show up for her grueling high school schedule (two classes, I think they were Poetry and Snowboard Making) and kept taking off at lunch to get stoned and what have you, the orders came down from on high that

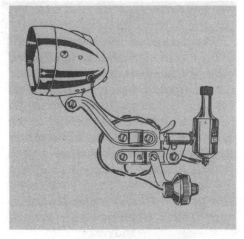

A generator used on a bicycle.

she was going to go to Gran's for lunch every day, since Gran's house was only about a three-minute walk from the high school.

The first couple of days Layla showed up at lunch and generally did as she was told. On the evening of day two, Dan asked Layla how her lunch at Gran's that day had been.

Layla was slumped sideways on the couch texting her boyfriend, the ne'er-do-well who would go on to father her child, and I use the word father fairly loosely here.

Layla took a deep breath and blurted out without pausing, "Lunch was terrible. Gran used moldy bread, I mean with actual green spots on it and everything, and she just cut the moldy bits off, but mold is spores, we learned about it in science, and spores they get on everything, you can't just cut off the green bits, it all still tastes like what it is, which is mold. And you know how she won't use real butter, so there was tons of margarine all over the bread and just barely any mayonnaise at all, like mayonnaise was made of gold or something. And the tomatoes, the tomatoes were clear. You could see right through them. Tomatoes are not naturally clear. You have to save them up for a long time before they get soft enough to be actually see-through. I just about gagged."

Now, I want to be clear here, that my cousin Dan is generally a fairly calm, cool, and amiable sort of guy. Suffice it to say by this point he had, as my gran herself was fond of saying, had it up to here with Layla. He exploded, his first finger drumming the air between him and his daughter.

"Are you fucking kidding me right at this minute? That old woman is nearly ninety years old, and her knees are shot and her teeth have all fallen out, and she is nearly blind and almost deaf as a post. She has a ruptured disc in her back and emphysema and di-verticulitis, and if she somehow manages to haul her ailing carcass up out of the hospital bed in the living room that she has to lie in now and hobble into that kitchen to fix you some lunch then you are going to eat every last single bite of whatever the fuck it is she puts in front of you and you are going to thank her and you are going to be grateful. AM I MAKING MYSELF CLEAR ENOUGH FOR YOU HERE OR WHAT?"

You know, and so forth.

Layla recoiled into the couch cushions, her mouth agape. Then she shut her mouth into a giant pout. "All right all right, you don't have to freak out at every little thing I say. God, why does my life SUCK SO MUCH?"

So the next day she shows back up at gran's just after noon. Gran was out on the deck, smashing out a Player's light regular butt into an overfull ashtray. She seemed chipper and upbeat, her wrinkled cheeks pink and ruddy in the cold.

Lunch that day was a classic. Grilled cheese and Campbell's tomato soup from a can. If you don't like grilled cheese and tomato soup then, well, I don't want to know you. And I can't even eat bread anymore, on account of the gluten. Or canned soup for that matter. But you know what I mean.

Anyway. Grilled cheese and tomato soup was one of Layla's favourites, so she slid into a chair and dug in.

But two bites into her grilled cheese Layla realized something was not right with that sandwich. A funny, chemical taste, she recounts to me much later. But the previous day's lecture still rung in her ears. So she sucked it up and ate her sandwich, swallowing and chewing each mouthful methodically, trying not to make any kind of a face and tip my gran off that she wasn't digging her lunch again. Plus, Gran had gotten someone to get a fresh loaf of bread, so she just stayed silent and chewed her weird sandwich like a champ. It wasn't until the very last bite, which she spun around to pop crust-first into her mouth, that she realized what the odd taste had been. My gran had forgotten to remove the plastic wrapper from the Kraft single before she fried it all up in her cast iron pan.

I found her will when I was going through some of her old papers, I almost missed it because in true Flo Daws fashion, it had been written on the back of a Yukon Electric hydro bill and stuffed into a recycled birthday card envelope with someone else's name on the front of it. In capital letters on the outside of that envelope Gran had scrawled, "This is my will. I know what I want, & please carry them out God Bless you all, Mum." My grandmother's last will and testament read, in point form: "Cheapest coffin. No flowers. All donations to Sacred Heart Cathedral & no tea afterwards. Lots of singing at the mass. And please, no fighting. And thank you God, for keeping us all together."

There was a postscript, in a different coloured ink, like an afterthought. "These are my last wishes. Please, carry them out. I will be watching."

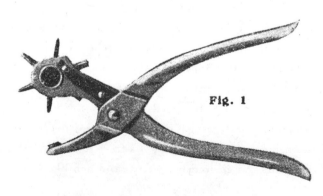

Fig. 1

# LONELY STRIPPER ON CHRISTMAS

My most vivid memory of the girls is bath night. The girls were what we called them, my little cousins Racheal and Lindsay, my mom's sister's two youngest kids. I was nearly fifteen when Racheal was born, and seventeen when Lindsay came along, so we were never kids together, and part of me will always only remember them as the girls. No matter how old we all manage to get, in some place in my head they will always be two scrawny little squeaky girls on bath night in Aunt Roberta's old house on Kennedy Street in Nanaimo.

My gran had this rule about clothes dryers being a luxury phenomenon, a shocking waste of good money that bred an inherent weakness into those lazy enough to use them, and Roberta believed it. We were a clothesline-only kind of family all the way, rain, shine, or forty below. But, sometimes on weeknights my aunts or my gran would go out to bingo, leaving me to babysit. We would lie around in our pajama pants, eat ripple chips and make iced tea ... and use the clothes dryer. I know. Such rebels.

The trick was to get the laundry in and folded and put away in time for the clothes dryer to cool before anyone got home from bingo and busted us for wasting electricity, a crime second only to throwing perfectly good food out when there were children starving in Africa, or leaving the front door open and heating the whole universe.

It must have been somewhere between drying the towels and folding them, still almost damp and warm, and stuffing them into the hallway linen closet that we got the idea for Kiddie Burrito.

Anyone who has ever had the first four layers of their skin sandpapered off by a threadbare towel straight off the old Yukon clothesline knows what a true luxury a fluffy towel fresh out of the clothes dryer really is.

The trick was all in the timing. Christopher and Dan, the girls' much older brothers, would wait downstairs, standing at the ready next to the rolling and rumbling clothes dryer, with the basement door propped open with a boot or something, until they got the signal from me. The signal was a yell, and this happened seconds before the little girls stepped out of the bath. The boys would whip two hot towels out of the dryer at the last possible minute and fling themselves up the stairs three at a time, then toss the towels to me. I would wrap Racheal and then Lindsay in huge hot-as-humanly-possible towels, their pencil-thin baby arms pinned at their sides, like little, well, kiddy burritos, and then proceed to squeeze them until they complained of not being able to breathe. "You're squishing all the air out of me," they would whine, but truth was, we all loved it. Inherent in this bliss was the following truth: small luxuries are never lost on the unspoiled.

Or, maybe we just all needed a better hobby?

Whatever the case, I will always remember those winter nights, the girls pink-cheeked and smelling like cheap apple-scented shampoo and sitting perfect in their clean jammies on the couch waiting for me to figure out exactly which of the much used VHS tapes crammed into the drawer under the television actually had the Saturday morning cartoons dubbed over somebody's old exercise video on it. Peeling scotch tape over the holes on the VHS cassette and ballpoint ink-chicken scratch that had once said JANE FONDA, now crossed off and replaced by BUGS BUNNY scrawled underneath it.

Little Lindsay ended up marrying a firefighter and works up at the hospital, a pushing paperwork kind of job, not pushing wheelchairs or meal trays or pills or a mop. Lindsay lived with our gran right up until she got married and moved in with Cameron, and more than any of us, she inherited through osmosis our gran's now notorious frugalness. Lindsay's bookshelves are empty on account of we have libraries full of free books, so who in their right mind would buy a book, and she started saving for her retirement before she graduated from high school, true story.

And Racheal, well Racheal takes after Racheal. After a brief career as a scantily clad lady mud-wrestler sponsored by a tequila company, she became a dancer. The gentleman's nightclub kind of dancer. She made down payments on designer handbags and three rounds of breast augmentations and majored in taking selfies, doting on miniature dogs and hairless cats, and reapplying her flawless lip liner at stoplights.

Nature versus nature. I love them both fiercely.

A couple of Christmases back, my partner at the time Zena and I made a promise to each other. We were going to spend the day just her and me, alone together. No travelling to visit friends or family, no big dinner to prepare, just her and me and the little dog on the couch. A no-pants day. I was going to make a shepherd's pie.

The only commitment I couldn't and wouldn't want to forgo was my family's custom of everybody calling everybody ridiculously early on Christmas morning. The phone is passed around and you say quick hellos to hungover uncles and technically second cousins whom we call nieces and nephews who are whipped into a sugar and new Barbie or snowboard-induced frenzy. This process takes about three hours, give or take. I have a big family. Zena had her mother, who was frail and then breathing with the help of an oxygen tank, so her single-mother-only-daughter salutations were over in minutes. This used to be a bit of an issue for us, until we got married and she grew to love the whole motley mess of us, and they started to demand that I pass the phone to her when they were finished with me. So we did the rounds. I called Racheal last, because I know she often works until last call at the bar.

I could tell as soon as she picked up that something was wrong. Her voice was more the little girl I remembered than it was the young woman she had become. She sounded small, and sad. Told me that her boyfriend, the rich Russian oil patch heir, was at a big family dinner, and that he couldn't take her. Subtext went unspoken but I heard it resounding in her somber silence. The boyfriend was loaded enough to have the stripper arm candy girlfriend, but it was too loaded to bring her to meet the relatives. My baby cousin was being covered up, like a long sleeve hiding a fading forearm tattoo, or an inheritance taking care of a gambling debt, or a low grade point average.

I looked over at Zena, who had been listening to my half of the conversation. I shrugged my shoulders to ask, can we? And she nodded yes, of course. I told Racheal that we would wait until she got here to start cooking the pancakes, and that she was staying for dinner, too. She said she would be over in an hour, sniffling a little in the background just before she hung up.

The three of us spent the better part of that Christmas day on our couch, in a swirl of blankets and pillows and bits of dropped potato chips. We told Zena all of our top twenty remember-the-time-when-we stories, and I played Racheal a recording of the song my friend Jon wrote for our gran and we cried until Racheal got mascara on the arm of my t-shirt.

I don't remember exactly what it was that Racheal said or when, we talked all day and well into that night, but I do recall at some point looking at the profile of her sweet face lit up from behind by the streetlights outside and realizing that the little girl I had known was now not only grown up, but grown into herself, somehow. That I, just like almost everyone, had failed to look past the false eyelashes and silicone of her and see the truth there. She was hilarious, and smart, and possessed just as much insight into the murky world of gender as either Zena or I did.

I have often wondered why my extremely devout grandmother never raised much of a Catholic eyebrow when it came to Racheal's choice of profession. My grandmother always just told Rachie to be smart with her money, to sock it away for a rainy day. Same thing she told all of us.

I walked Racheal out to her car that night. Hugged her under a streetlight. It was starting to rain a little. I watched as the windshield wipers blurred her face and then squeaked for more rain. She was tapping her iPhone with a bejeweled fingernail, and its blue screen lit up her features in a glowing square. She looked older than her twenty-six years should have let her look, and a little lonely. She blew me a kiss and her taillights blinked goodbye at me when she turned the corner.

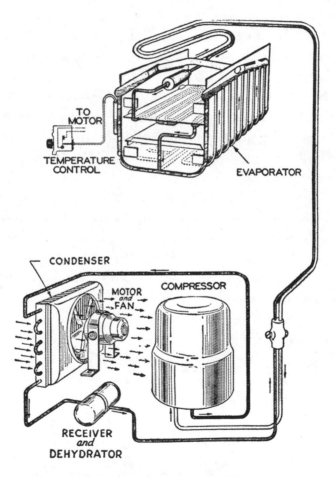

TO MOTOR

TEMPERATURE CONTROL

EVAPORATOR

CONDENSER

MOTOR and FAN

COMPRESSOR

RECEIVER and DEHYDRATOR

# A CIRCLE GOES ROUND

My grandmother was prone to strange acts of ritual; she routinely performed them and taught us all to do likewise. None of us questioned these habits until we got much older. She would throw a pinch of salt over her left shoulder with her right hand if she had spilled any, and we were forbidden to hang pictures of living people up on the walls, in case the picture should fall down and bring death with it. Our school photos were framed and leaned against the wall on the mantle, or on top of the bureau, never hung up. Hanging pictures of already dead people was acceptable. We were not allowed to ever place a hat on a bed, and if you gave someone a purse or a wallet as a gift you had to put a shiny penny in it, or you were dooming them to bad financial luck. No empty wallets, and no questions. This is just what you did.

I guess we thought it was all Catholic stuff, and yours is not to wonder why, yours is just to do or die, as the saying goes. It wasn't until I started interviewing her in 2003 for what my family had taken to calling "my little art projects" that she began to show us the dusty corners of her life story. She had been told to lie about who she was. It was not a good idea to be part Irish and part Roma in London, England during Hitler's rise to power and the Second World War. It was better to just be an English girl, even a poor one, and so that is what she always said she was. Fear of being the other. The unwanted. The disposable. One of the greatest tools for forced conformity we have ever invented. Powerful enough to sustain a lie across an ocean and through generations. Even in the last years of her life, tucked safely into her chair at the end of the kitchen table with a cup of tea, the truth still came out in little fits and starts. And

I was there to hear it and save it from the past.

My gran had a New Year's Eve ritual she taught us all, maybe it was a Roma thing passed down to her from her secret people, I don't know. She would take one stick of firewood, a fistful of silver dimes she would sock away all year in a Crown Royal bag in the drawer of the bureau in the hall (they were real silver back then, dimes were, remember?), silver candlesticks, her turquoise and silver ring (anything silver), and one loaf of bread. Just after midnight at least one person was selected, usually an unmarried young man, I think with brown hair, to lead a contingent of revelers in a run outside

Fig. 10

around the house three times, clockwise, carrying these items. I would join them, sometimes with my parka on over my pajamas, following my mom and aunties, who were drunk on white wine or maybe gin-and-tonics, slipping on the ice and laughing until Deb Walsh from up the road peed a little in her gabardine pantsuit, thirty below and our breaths growing into ice on our eyelashes. Later, as a preteen, I would run wearing just a Lee Storm Rider jeans jacket or sometimes a Levis one, and bald tennis shoes and no mitts or scarf because I thought it was cool, we all thought it was cool, then later still, drunk myself or stoned on mushrooms, and then later, as a young person out on my own, around my beat-up but beloved rented attic suite that burned down, fourteen years I ran around that house until it was no more.

The firewood is for warmth, and a safe roof, shelter. The silver is for prosperity, and good work given and done. The bread is for your table, and the wish is may you break it and share it with loved ones. You run to conjure these things up, to invite warmth and wealth and plenty into your new year.

A few years ago my partner at the time Zena and I threw a party on New Year's Eve. I hadn't been planning it, but at about nine p.m. I called my friend Cynthia, who has a fireplace, and asked her to bring a couple of prime pieces of kindling with her. I inherited my grandmother's love of the pre-1968 silver dime, so I had a couple stashed away. I stuffed them into a faded Crown Royal bag with some candlesticks, an antique spoon, and some jewelry. A leaden loaf of gluten free sunflower seed and flax bread was procured from the freezer. Just before midnight I gathered a few folks game enough to come and run with me.

I had never run around a roof I owned before. It is a very small roof, connected to a lot of other people's roofs, and I won't truly own it for another twenty years or so, but still. When we stepped out of the lobby onto the sidewalk I realized that this wasn't going to be three drunken loops around a single family dwelling like the good old days. It was going to be three pretty much sober laps of the entire block, because we were living in a fifty-seven-suite building attached on all sides to the buildings next to it.

So we ran. On high heels and patent leather flats and in my good Fleuvog boots, hiking up sequined skirts and holding boobs and wigs and wallet chains in place, carrying silver and wood and bread. Two writers, an installation artist, a gender sciences researcher, a PhD candidate, a librarian, a boxer, and a longshorewoman ran past the bakery and the laundromat, around the corner store and through the smell of alley and dumpster, waved at the ladies working the parking lot outside of the 7-Eleven and laughed with the two drunk guys on the bus stop bench. Me with my gran's blood in my veins, rushing in warm beats past my eardrums, trying not to puke up the duck confit and shitake mushroom gravy poutine we all had just eaten.

I could feel my grandmother with me, all around us. We all piled into the elevator, breathless and blood-cheeked and leaning on each other we were laughing so hard, and I felt my grandmother whisper into my ear. You want to know what she said, what she whispered across the bridge of ritual and tradition to me from the great beyond?

Whatsa matter with you running around in your good boots like that? You want to ruin them being foolish, do you? Don't be vain. Next time wear your sneakers. That's what they're made for.

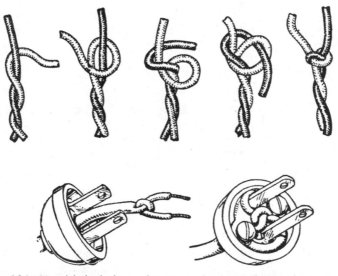

**Figs. 24 to 30.**—Method of tying knot in appliance cord and wire attachment to binding screws on plug.

# "SHOULD" ALL OVER EVERYONE

My aunt called me today. She's only eleven years older than me. We had a really good chat. She has had a rough couple of years; two Septembers ago her husband died in his sleep of a massive heart attack, and then a couple of weeks later she was diagnosed with breast cancer.

"My mom sent me the breast cancer survivor calendar you were in," I told her. "When I opened it up to January, there you were. You looked so beautiful and strong, it choked me right up."

She told me how much she hated that picture, that she couldn't believe it was the one the photographer had picked to use.

"I think that photographer looked right inside of you and caught your strength. The part of you that survived everything," I told her, and I heard her let out a long breath. Took a drag off of her cigarette. I could see her in my mind, her feet stuffed into her baby blue fuzzy slippers and her fleece jacket pulled over her shoulders, smoking a Player's Light Regular on her back porch with the sliding door pulled shut behind her. The barbecue covered up since Kevin died, and blanketed now in December snow. The birdfeeder hanging from the big pine tree next to the railing on the deck. The sun gone already and the moon bouncing off of all that quiet white in her back yard. The world behind her silent except for ravens gurgling back and forth on the power line.

"I read your book *Gender Failure*," she said, changing the subject. "It took me a while because I could only read a chapter at a time, and then put it down and then go back a couple of days later."

"Why's that?" I held the phone between my chin and collarbone so I could unlock the front door of my building.

"It made me feel so guilty."

"Guilty? I never meant for it to make anyone feel guilty. Why guilty?"

"There are so many things I should have seen, that I could have known, if I had been paying any kind of attention at all. I had no idea, but I should have known." I heard her exhale, then take another long drag.

"How could you have known? I didn't even know. I didn't even figure myself out until just a couple of years ago. I could have told you more. I should have talked to you more. I just didn't even have the words yet myself. I'm getting in the elevator now," I tell her. "If I lose you I'll call you right back, okay?"

"I could have asked. How many thoughtless things have I said? I can't even think about it now."

We both went quiet for a minute. I was alone in the elevator. I could feel the tears coming. I blinked them away.

"Promise me if I ever say something stupid or hurtful, you will tell me," she blurted out. "I'm just learning. You're still the only trans person that I know."

"Only if you promise me the same thing," I told her, dropping my keys on the counter and bending to untie my bootlaces and kick them off. I pushed a kitchen chair away from the table with my knee and sat down. It was cold in my apartment, and the little dog wandered over to say hello, his toenails clicking a rhythm on the hardwood floor.

"That's a promise," my aunt said softly into the phone, and I heard her slide the glass door open and then shut it again. "You know I love you so much."

"I love you too," I told her. "And Merry Christmas."

"I'm just so glad it's over for another year," she said, and I nodded, even though I knew she couldn't see me.

"When are you going to quit smoking?" I asked her.

"When hells freezes over." She laughed. "Actually, if hell freezes over, then I'm going to smoke my face off. No sense quitting for the end of the world."

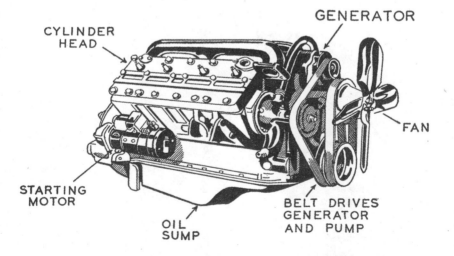

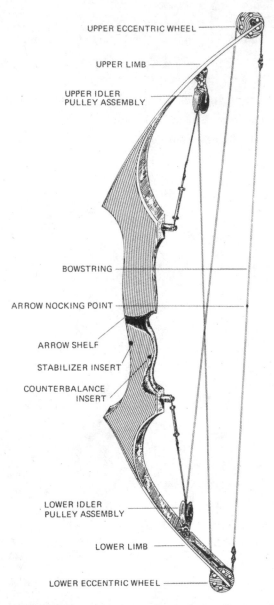

UPPER ECCENTRIC WHEEL

UPPER LIMB

UPPER IDLER
PULLEY ASSEMBLY

BOWSTRING

ARROW NOCKING POINT

ARROW SHELF

STABILIZER INSERT

COUNTERBALANCE
INSERT

LOWER IDLER
PULLEY ASSEMBLY

LOWER LIMB

LOWER ECCENTRIC WHEEL

**NEW COMPOUND BOWS** have the latest refinements in accessories plus significant mechanical advantage.

# MIDDLE SEAT

It's hard for me to describe to those of you who have always felt comfortable and seen in the gender box you were placed in at birth what it feels like when someone refers to you by the wrong pronoun. It is not enough for me to just ask the men in the room what it would feel like to constantly be called a lady, or for the women in the room to imagine being called sir when you were all dressed up for a day at work. If you have not struggled to fit into and/or escape from your assigned gender box, then you cannot truly know what this feels like. If passing as your chosen gender has never been a matter of safety or danger for you, a matter of being respected or reviled, then you cannot and will not truly understand me, but I will attempt to describe it to you anyway. Imagine a world full of strangers who all have a tiny little razor in their hands and they can randomly, mostly accidentally, shave a tiny piece of your soul off you while they sell you a newspaper or pass you the key to the bathroom at the gas station. Now imagine your classmates and co-workers have an even bigger blade, and can cut deeper. Imagine your friends and family members wield a really big knife. Imagine that all of these cuts can whittle away at the flesh of you, day after day after day, rendering the truth of you into a sliver, almost invisible, unrecognizable. Imagine that these cuts sting for hours afterwards, sometimes days, and that they tend to fester. Imagine that you have to get through every day, bleeding from hundreds of wounds, some little and some deep, all the while pretending that nothing hurts.

I would like to phase out the use of the phrase "prefers the pronoun" she or he or they, (or any other) and replace it with "uses the pronoun." I prefer chicken to duck. I prefer a window seat. But I use the pronoun they. When someone writes that a person "prefers" a particular pronoun, it implies that there is a choice there for everyone whether to respect that wish or not, and that the person with the pronoun "preference" would be okay with the middle seat or the duck of their identity being respected. Not true. For some (if not most) gender variant and/or trans folks, not having their pronoun respected is hurtful, and constantly correcting people is exhausting and alienating. So I vow to change my language. People don't prefer their chosen pronoun, they use it. My only choice is to be mindful and respectful of others, or to be thoughtless and even cruel. This is not to say I get it right all the time every time, but that is my aim. Saying things like, "But I find it so hard to remember because we grew up together," is a cop-out. If you grew up together, then you owe it to the person to do better by them. And if you want to try the "but the they pronoun is so awkward" angle with me, then I would ask you to think about how your struggle compares to the battles trans people have to fight every day.

# BABY STRONG

I don't remember for sure who called me first. I think maybe it was my mom.

"I need to ask you a favour." She was using her down-low, it's-a-serious-thing voice. I sat up straighter at my kitchen table. "We've got a situation brewing up here. I need you to call Danny and ask him to reconsider his stance on this whole baby shower thing. Don't tell him I told you to."

"What baby shower thing?" I asked her, taking a long breath and letting it out slow. My family has weird customs regarding the sharing of knowledge, for some reason they seem to prefer that everyone promise not to tell anyone they said anything about anything, ever, all the while knowing that they just told the person least likely or able to keep their mouth shut a secret that half of them already knew from hearing it from someone else who was also supposed to keep it to themselves on a need to know basis. It all quickly gets hard to keep track of, especially once removed from the thick of it, and it can be frustrating. Especially when I do manage to keep my mouth shut about something and then no one else except the original leak mentions anything about it to me again, and so I don't hear the news updates about important shit because either everybody assumed someone had already told me, or they didn't want to be the first one to let the cat out of the bag because they think I'm the one who can't keep a secret.

My mother cleared her throat. I could hear her stirring her mug with her teaspoon. Probably some kind of fancy rooibos. Mocha mint or something.

"Well you know that Robert and Christine are having a baby. So they're having a baby shower next week. I should probably let Danny tell you the rest."

"But you're not going to." I smiled to myself and waited.

"Well, they decided to have a gender party."

Now, if this were my queer friends having a gender party in East Vancouver, I might have busted out a mascara moustache or borrowed someone's high heels and gotten into it. But it was my cousin the brew master in the Yukon and his pregnant girlfriend throwing this particular gender party, so something told me there was more than one kind of gender party out there and the gender party in question might not be what had initially sprung to my mind.

"What's a gender party exactly, Mom?" I asked, not quite sure I really wanted to know.

She started talking fast like she had just been waiting for me to ask what she had just told me she wasn't going to talk about. "The expectant parents go to the bakery and get a cake made up. Or I guess they could bake it at home. Whatever. They dye the cake pink inside if the baby is a girl, or they make a blue cake for a boy, and then they cover it with icing, like regular icing, to hide the colour of the cake. Then they throw a party, like a kind of baby shower I guess, and when they cut into the cake, then they reveal to everyone what sex the baby is."

"So we can start its indoctrination?" I ask.

"Don't start with that. It's supposed to be a party," she says. I can feel her furrowing her brow at me all the way from the Yukon Territory. "Call your cousin, please. Your poor aunt Nora is upset about it all. Her first grandchild. After what happened with Kevin."

Here is where I explain it all to folks who don't have thirty-six cousins, fourteen aunts, and twelve uncles. Danny is my cousin. My mom's nephew. My cousin Dan didn't want to go to the gender party of the unborn child of my other cousin Robert, and Robert's mom was my aunt Nora, also known as my mom's youngest sister. Nora was still reeling from the recent and unexpected death of her husband, my uncle Kevin, whose heart exploded in his sleep just months before he would have should have met his first grandchild, the baby whose gender was about to be announced to the family via the inside colour of a store-bought cake.

I did what I was told and called my cousin Dan.

"It's ridiculous," he says over the speakerphone in his car. "I was like, come on, people? A gender party? Has anyone thought about how this would feel for Ivan? It's the year 2013, why do we even need to know what gender the kid is? Why, so we can all start leaning over Christine's belly and whispering to it that it isn't going to be good at math or can't be a fireman when it grows up? That it shouldn't cry in public? I'm not going, you know, just on principle."

But somewhere Dan must have changed his mind, because he did end up going to the gender party, which is how the following happened:

I think they had the party at my Aunt Nora's place, because she has the biggest living room. So all my cousins from my mom's side are there, and a couple from my dad's side too, and a couple of my aunts and uncles, and Ed and Elaine, Kevin's parents, the great-grandparents to be. Someone probably put out some chips in a bowl with ranch or dill pickle dip, and a veggie tray and some cold cuts. There were cigarettes smoked and extinguished in the over-full ashtray on the back deck, and then someone turned the sound down on the flat screen but left the picture on in the living room, and everyone gathered around the big table in the dining room. Christine complained about her sore lower back and then leaned over and cut the cake. Laid the serrated knife on its side and used the blade to lift a wedge of pink cake with white icing onto a dessert plate, and everyone cheered.

"It's a girl!" my Aunt Nora exclaimed, tears brimming in her blue eyes. Someone passed her a square of paper towel and she folded it in half and dabbed at her running mascara.

"For now!" my cousin Dan said loudly, and the room went silent.

Amelia Pearl Kevin was born at the end of January, nearly three weeks overdue. She bears the names of her great grandmothers and the grandfather who already loved her but never got to hold her. Legend has it she was born already able to hold her head up, and one of the first times she was placed on her belly she did a half push-up in protest.

Robert, her father, was one of the younger kids born to our generation, and he didn't change a lot of diapers and watch a lot of toddlers grow up, so he wasn't as familiar with the development of babies as some of us are.

When the new parents took their newborn in to the health nurse to be weighed and have her check-up, Robert mentioned that he thought the baby was pretty strong for her age.

The nurse let out a snort and smiled at the young couple. "Pretty strong?" she laughed and shook her head. "Your baby has oblique muscles."

I met her for the first time when she was ten months old, still bald as an apple, threatening to stand straight up from a seated position, and nearly walking. Terrifying everyone by tirelessly climbing long flights of stairs as fast as she could, looking over her shoulder to make certain someone was watching and that they were suitably impressed with her.

I chatted with my aunt Nora as she changed her diaper one afternoon. Amelia wouldn't even lie flat on her back, instead she sat half-upright in a kind of Pilates V, her little muscles all flexed like she was multi-tasking, getting a quick ab workout in until such time as she could change her own diaper. Staring intently at her grandmother, like she was timing the whole operation, or going to write up a full report on the experience later.

I didn't say it, but I held it there on the tip of my tongue. That's what you get for having a gender party, I thought to myself, and said nothing.

"Everybody calls her Baby Strong," Nora confessed, and we both laughed.

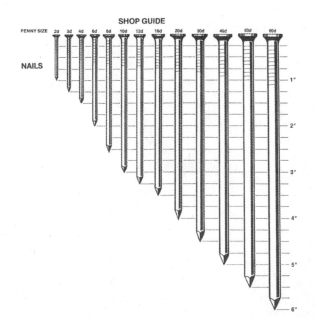

My new shirt. Plaid on the outside, but with flowers on the inside.
Just like me.

# VUL-NER-A-BLE

I get off the airplane and come down the airport escalator, looking for a person who looks like they are looking for me.

I had received an email the day before from the writer's festival saying someone would be at the airport to pick me up, but they didn't give me a name, or tell me what this person looked like.

But I see her, she has long curly brown hair and I see her step forward, raising a gloved hand to wave at me. She offers to take my suitcase, but I tell her it's cool, I've got it. We head out through the automatic doors, through a cloud of cigarette smoke coming from a gaggle of baggage handlers next to the taxi stand, and head for the parking garage.

It is cold here, much colder than it is in Vancouver, and I am glad I wore the down parka and packed my mitts and scarf.

She apologizes that the heater is not working very well in her car, and proceeds to scrape the frost off the inside of her windshield. The back seat of her aging Honda Civic hatchback is a mishmash of festival programs, a hairy dog blanket, a kid's booster seat, someone's mittens, a duffle bag, empty coffee mugs, and a Thighmaster. An actual Thighmaster. I wonder for a minute how it ended up in the back seat of her car, but don't ask.

She works for the festival. Probably on contract, and she probably has two or three other jobs to make it all work. Today is the second day of a seven-day festival. She most likely has eleven other tasks to take care of before she picks up her kid at daycare at five. It's 3:50 p.m. but the clock on the dash of her car reads 4:50 p.m. because she hasn't set it back since daylight savings time happened six weeks ago. She has received four texts already since we got in the car; we haven't even hit the freeway yet. She tries not to look at her phone because she is driving, but glances at it at stoplights.

We leave the freeway and pull over into the parking lot of an Esso station. She gets out and puts some air into the rear passenger tire, climbs back in, and programs the hotel address into her cell phone's GPS.

"Four years here but I still can't figure out the one-way streets downtown," she tells me. Then takes a big breath.

"I want you to know how much your books have meant to me. I read them in college when I was coming out. I gave them to my folks. I made my little brother read them. And it wasn't just the queer content thing. It was the small town stuff. Your family. So much queer writing is all big-city-estranged-from-your-family-punk-rock stuff. Your books were the first queer stories I read where I could actually see myself in them."

We were pulling into the little loop of a driveway in front of the hotel. There was a small bench there, and an ashtray full of white sand and a frozen tree in a large pot. A worn red all-season carpet.

"Anyways. I wanted to thank you for making yourself so vulnerable. That's what I always wonder when I read your work, what must it be like, to be so honest, so ... wide open?"

She shook her head, smiled at me. She looked tired. "Anyway. I hope this doesn't make you feel weird. I'm excited to see you read tonight. Someone will be here at around quarter to seven to walk you over to the theatre. All the writers are meeting in the lobby just before then."

I checked into my hotel room, took a shower, ironed my shirt, and then stretched out on the lonely king-sized bed, opened up my laptop, and wrote:

I get asked what it feels like to write such vulnerable things. What it feels like to make myself vulnerable like that, to lay myself and my life on the page like that. Isn't it scary?

Yes. It is scary to write about private, painful things. It is terrifying, sometimes. Sometimes the only way I can make myself finish a sentence is to tell myself that no one will ever read it. To promise myself that I can erase that line immediately as soon as it is out of my head if I need to. Sometimes I do this. I often cry when I write about difficult things, and feel the words heavy in me and on me after, sometimes for a couple of days. I worry what my mother will think. I wonder if I got it right, I worry that the reader will not take my words with the same heart that I had when I wrote them, I fret that I have left something out or that I've said nothing new. I lie in bed at night and deep breathe through the fear of my new words going out there on their shaky legs to be interpreted, critiqued, weighed, and displayed.

But I don't feel vulnerable. Writing about vulnerable things doesn't make me feel vulnerable. Writing about my tenderest bits is the only way I know how to have power over them. Staying silent would leave me alone with them. My silence is what makes me vulnerable. My secrets are sharpest when I am the only one holding them. Writing them down turns all my secrets into something else. Something closer to strength.

I flew home a couple of days later, and I'm still thinking about this now. I look up the definition of vulnerable.

vul·ner·a·ble. It's an adjective. It means to be susceptible to physical or emotional attack or harm. Or in the case of a person, in need of special care, support, or protection because of age, disability, or risk of abuse or neglect. Its synonyms are helpless, defenseless, powerless, impotent, weak, and susceptible.

Writing down difficult things has never made me any of those things.

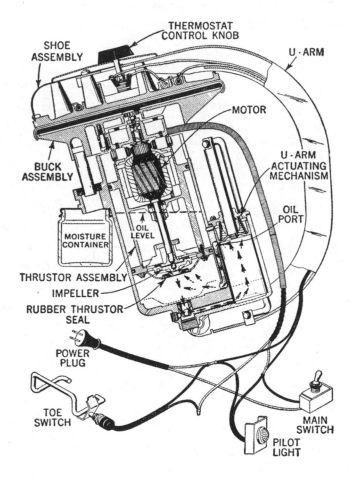

THERMOSTAT
CONTROL KNOB

SHOE
ASSEMBLY

U · ARM

MOTOR

U · ARM
ACTUATING
MECHANISM

BUCK
ASSEMBLY

OIL
PORT

MOISTURE
CONTAINER

OIL
LEVEL

THRUSTOR ASSEMBLY

IMPELLER

RUBBER THRUSTOR
SEAL

POWER
PLUG

TOE
SWITCH

MAIN
SWITCH

PILOT
LIGHT

# UNCOMFORTABLE

*com·fort·a·ble*

> I looked it up. It's an adjective and
> it means
> providing physical ease and relaxation.
> or
> physically relaxed and free from constraint.
> Comfortable.
> It means not in pain and
> free from stress or fear,
> free from hardship
> or,
> as large as is needed or wanted.

A couple of years ago I published a piece on Slate.com about gender-neutral bathrooms. I get hassled a lot in public bathrooms, so, you know, I thought it might be nice to not get hassled in bathrooms. It was the first time any of my writing had gone out to a largely straight, high-traffic, fairly mainstream online audience. They published a full-colour picture of me, too. I didn't get paid. I did it for the, you know, exposure.

I was alone on a Greyhound bus in Alberta on tour when my piece went live. It started with a rumble in the stomach of my social media, and quickly barfed its way into my email inbox. My words, my name, and my contact information had been posted nearly simultaneously on a right-wing evangelical pray-the-gay-away website, and a radical lesbian separatist website run by women who spelled women with a Y and didn't want to share anything with trans people, ever.

You're getting lots of hits, my publicist texted me. Just don't read the comments. But I did read the emails.

It was, how do I put it, illuminating? How many times I had to re-read those emails to see who was writing, to be sure whether it was a born-again Christian or a womyn-born-womyn, who had written what exactly.

And two songs remained eerily the same, repeated in many different ways, over and over, by both seemingly ideologically opposite groups. But both of them said:

No offense, but, if I had to share a woman's washroom with someone who looks like you, I would feel ... uncomfortable.

And ...

Why don't you just use the men's room?

Both sides drawing pictures of different kinds of monsters that sort of look like me. Both sides unsure where to put the possibility of me. But I just need to pee.

I didn't answer most of them then, so I will answer them now. First off, any statement that begins with "no offense, but ..." is the ass-crack-smelling handshake of all sentence structure. I mean, it seems friendly enough, but it always leaves you sniffing the air afterwards, and wondering.

If all the born-again Christians think I should just use the men's room, then why do they keep passing laws saying I have to use the bathroom God gave me when he made me a girl?

And if the trans exclusive radical feminists say they don't feel safe with people who have or once had a penis in the women's bathroom, then why do they assume I would be safe in the men's room without one?

Both sides selling out my safety for their ... comfort?

They say they are afraid of men in the women's washroom because of what might happen. But I'm afraid of women in the women's washroom because of what happens to me all the time.

Meanwhile there is still not one single recorded case of a trans person assaulting anyone, ever, in a public bathroom of any variety. Believe me, when a trans person needs to use a public bathroom we are in and out of there faster than any of you can say, "But I didn't even get to see their genitals."

But mostly here's what I want to know:

Who the hell decides who gets to feel comfortable?

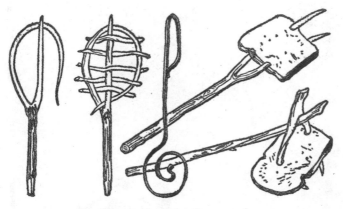

**Broilers and sticks for toasting**

Flagging has never gone out. Should never, ever be allowed to go out. May all the secret languages of the queers and the bent live on in our pockets forever.

# LEARN PEOPLE BETTER

Some people like to call it eavesdropping. I prefer to think of it as following Woody Guthrie's new year's resolutions for 1942. Right between "Listen to Radio A Lot" and "Don't Get Lonesome," he promises to "Learn People Better." So, some might call it eavesdropping, but me, I try to listen to everything anyone within my earshot says whenever I walk anywhere, just so I can learn people better.

The other day I was waiting at a stoplight close to a school. There was a girl talking to a boy, having a heated discussion. They were both about eleven years old. She was obviously pretty upset; he looked a little sheepish, dragging the toes of his running shoes along the sidewalk. "You just can't treat me like this," she told him, both hands on her hips. "I just won't have it." The boy looked down. Said nothing. Just nodded.

The other day I was walking behind two men, one in his mid-fifties, steel-toed boots, working man's hands. The other in his early twenties, sneakers, headphones around his neck. New York City. The older guy says, "She's mad because she thinks you're telling her how to solve things. She doesn't want you to solve it for her, she just wants you to listen to her. That is all most women want, is for you to just listen to them. Sooner you learn that the ..." He pauses, looks sideways at the kid. "Jesus, man, you're not even listening to me. What the fuck?"

The kid hitches his stride a bit, sighs. "I was. I was listening."

"Then what was I saying to you just now?"

Kid says nothing. Lets out a long breath. Shakes his head.

The older guy stops walking. Smacks the kid's shoulder with the backs of his fingertips. The kid shrugs, pulls his pants up by his belt.

"Well, if I listened to everything you told me every time you were talking to me, there would be no time left over for me to do any thinking."

Last Sunday on my way into Templeton Pool for trans-inclusive family swim, I pass by two kids kicking a soccer ball around, both about eight years old. The kid in the red shirt is guarding the street hockey net, the kid in the striped shirt is taking shots. Striped shirt boots the ball really hard and nails red shirt right in the face with it.

"Owwwww." Red shirt is trying not to let the tears escape his eyelids. "You fag. That hurt."

The kid in the striped shirt traps the rebound under his toe and stands up straight, his face stark and solemn. "Dude. I'm sorry I hit you in the face but you can't call people a fag anymore."

"Why not?" Red shirt is still pissed, squinting into the sun.

"Because. Like I already told you. I'm pretty sure my mom is a fag."

And then, today, came a chance to teach people better. Be better.

I'm on the phone with a credit card customer service woman:

"Royal Bank Visa, and how may I help you?"

"I have legally changed my name and I want to update my credit card," I tell her.

"What is the reason for the name change?"

I pause for a minute, considering. "I'm transgender."

"Okay!" she exclaims, like I just told her I had a baby or got married. "That's excellent."

"Most days it really is."

"I learn something new here every day," she says. I like the sound of her voice.

"Do you really?" I ask.

"Well, no, not really. But I'm going to today."

# WRITE THROUGH

I write through missing you. I think about you but write about other things.

I didn't wash my sheets for four days after you left. Found one of your hairs on a pillowcase, another in the bathtub, another tucked between the couch and a cushion. Could not bring myself to throw them in the garbage so I threw them off the balcony, letting gravity and the wind take them from my open hand.

In that liminal space between dreams and not quite conscious you come to me, I can feel your hand on my hip, my cheek, the top of my head, the soft spot at the base of my throat. I can smell you still on the handkerchief you embroidered for me. I tucked it into my suitcase just now, careful not to get too much of the smell of me on it because it has to last me for thirty more days. Sometimes I unfold it and hold it up to my cheek and just breathe.

I whisper my secret name for you three times into the dark before I close my eyes every night.

You said you saw me years ago and were just waiting for me to come around. You wouldn't tell me what year it was, but you said you were glad when I quit smoking cigarettes. That it meant it was closer to the right time for us. That was going on eight years ago. I smile when I do this math.

At the airport I saw you before I saw you. Something in your walk, moving just so through the businessmen on their phones and the lady with the stroller. I couldn't make my feet move and you laughed at me. No checked bags. I'm still impressed by that. Fresh lipstick at eleven o'clock at night and a dress I had not seen you wear yet.

You won't eat anything that comes out of a microwave. I have started heating the dog's food up on the stove in a tiny saucepan, just in case you are right about them.

I am changed already, I can feel it.

I have never seen you angry. You say you don't get angry much and I am starting to believe you. Even that night. You could have gotten mad but you didn't. We both cried and pulled it all apart with only our softest words in the dawn. Started fresh the next morning. When I woke up after we slept for a while I looked at you and I knew.

I could be safe here, I thought, and felt my chest ripped open with all that hope escaping me. You slept right through my epiphany and the word love nearly fell out of my mouth fifty times that day.

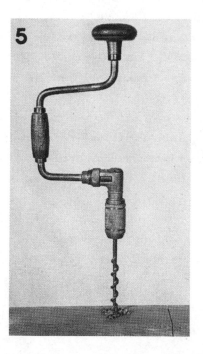

# HEAT AND HOT WATER

Tell me again how you love the half she and part he of me.

Show me with your mouth and hands and hips that there is no lonely bit of skin of mine untouched. Untraveled. Unseen.

Let me take that bag for you. I've got this, baby. I've got this.

Let me hang up your coat and put the kettle on.

Let my fingers find that spot on your neck that always hurts.

Let me.

I washed the sheets before you got here. Come here so I can remind myself of the smell of your neck and save it for later.

My jet-lagged love. Missing you is my only constant thing.

In the smallest hours I will wake up and remember that I get four more nights of you.

You will slip your warm hand around my middle and move me in your sleep.

You wake up before me because the day is half gone already in Toronto.

Even my dog can't take his eyes off of you dancing in my kitchen.

You smile that smile you save for me and tell me not to put a shirt on so you can watch me make your coffee.

Just like this, you say.

Just like this.

## 3 BLADE STOCKMAN'S POCKET KNIFE

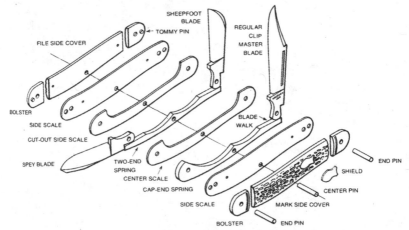

# WHAT WE PRAY FOR (THE TOMBOY HYMN)

```
C    G/B   C
```
To play the drums
```
        F   C/F  G
```
To be picked for teams
```
   C    C/F    C
```
A safe place to pee
```
      Em      Am
```
Tall trees to climb
```
   F  C/E  G
```
A dark blue bike
```
      C    G    C
```
For her to notice me

```
      E
```
Don't braid my hair
```
        Am
```
Don't make me wear
```
        G
```
That bridesmaid's dress, oh joy
```
      C   G/B   C
```
That school today
```
        F   C/E  G
```
Will be easy I pray
```
        C      G     C
```
Or to just wake up a boy

C
(Muscles, muscles, muscles, muscles, muscles, muscles, muscles)
C
Thou shalt learn to wink
     G
Thou shalt learn all the knots
     F
Thou shalt cuss liberally
        C
Thou shalt not trash talk
  G
the girls
           F
Thou shalt not let the world
make you hard
              C
Thou shalt learn to dance and lead

C
(Muscles, muscles, muscles, muscles, muscles, muscles, muscles)
C
Thou shalt acquire scars
      G
Thou shalt start a pine cone war
      F
Thou shalt practice throwing punches
     C
Thou shalt not wear a skort
   G
Get dirty

                  **F**
In your pockets thou shalt keep
A special rock a pocket knife your grubby mitts
               **C**
And several melodies


**G**

Tomboy! Tomboy! Tomboy!
**F**         **Dm**  **G**    **C**
Tomboy! Tomboy! Tomboy!


(Muscles, muscles, muscles, muscles, muscles, muscles, muscles)
(repeating)
  **C**
I always have a piece of string
  **G**
I want to practice French kissing
  **F**
Don't cry so much all of the time
  **G**
I shine my armour every night


  **G**

Tomboy! Tomboy! Tomboy!
**F**         **Dm**  **G**    **C**
Tomboy! Tomboy! Tomboy!

C
Thou shalt learn to wink

 G
Thou shalt learn all the knots
     F
Thou shalt cuss liberally
       C
Thou shalt not trash talk
   G
the girls
          F
Thou shalt not let the world

make you hard

make you bad
           C
Thou shalt learn to dance and lead

G
Tomboy! Tomboy! Tomboy!
F        Dm G   C
Just to be a good Tomboy!

"Who was I now—woman or man? That question could never be answered as long as those were the only choices; it could never be answered if it had to be asked."

—Leslie Feinberg

# ACKNOWLEDGMENTS

I would like to thank Arsenal Pulp Press for their continued vision and support of queer and trans writers. I am always proud to look over the list of new books they publish every season, and to witness their stalwart belief in publishing marginalized voices. They publish the kind of books I need to read, and for that I am ever grateful to Brian Lam, Robert Ballantyne, Oliver McPartlin, Susan Safyan, and the best-dressed publicist in Canadian publishing, Cynara Geissler. I thank them all for their continued commitment and integrity. I am proud to be an Arsenalian, and consider myself lucky to share a publisher with so many smart and talented artists and thinkers.

I would also like to thank my family for their unconditional love and support. We are able to have the hard discussions, and bend and break and grow and forgive, and then love each other better, and I think this makes me one of the luckiest people I know.

Photo: Jourdan Tymkow

IVAN COYOTE is the award-winning author or co-author of ten books and the creator of four short films as well as three CDs that combine storytelling with music. Ivan is a seasoned stage performer and an audience favourite at storytelling, literary, film, and folk music festivals as well as schools. Ivan lives in Vancouver.

*ivanecoyote.com*

# How to Tie Some Useful Knots

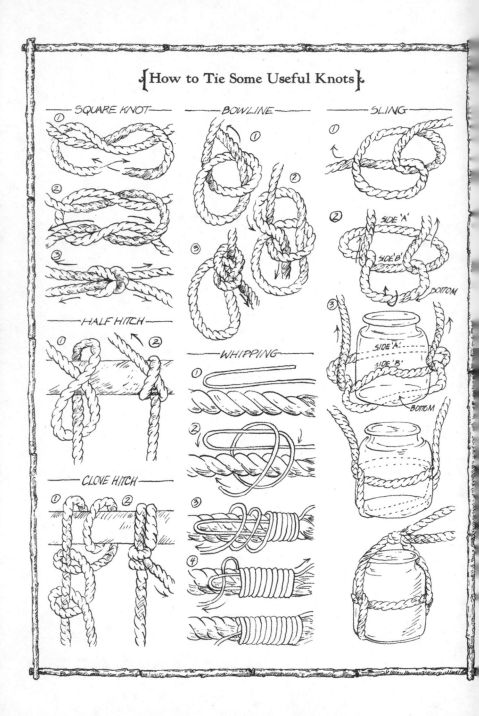

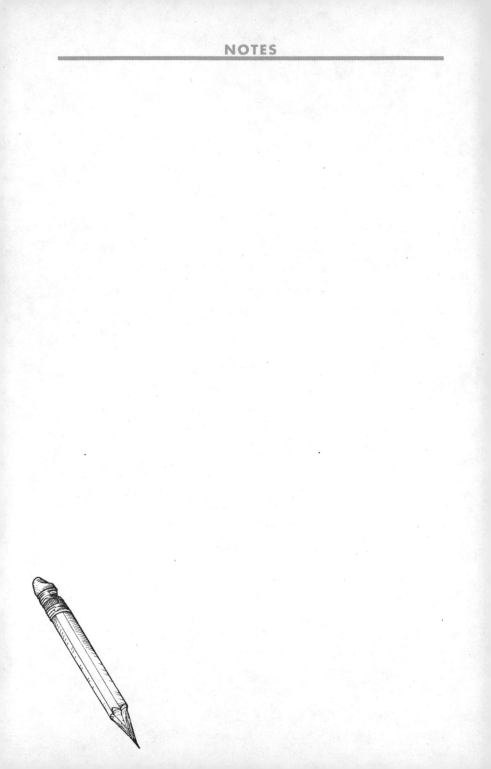

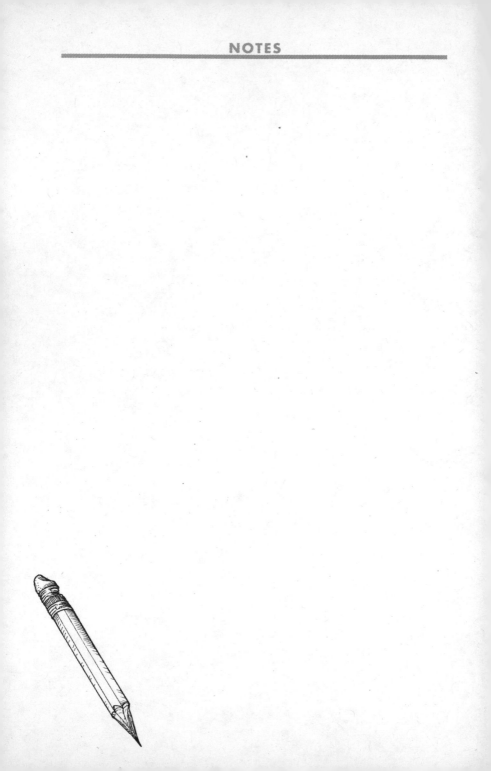

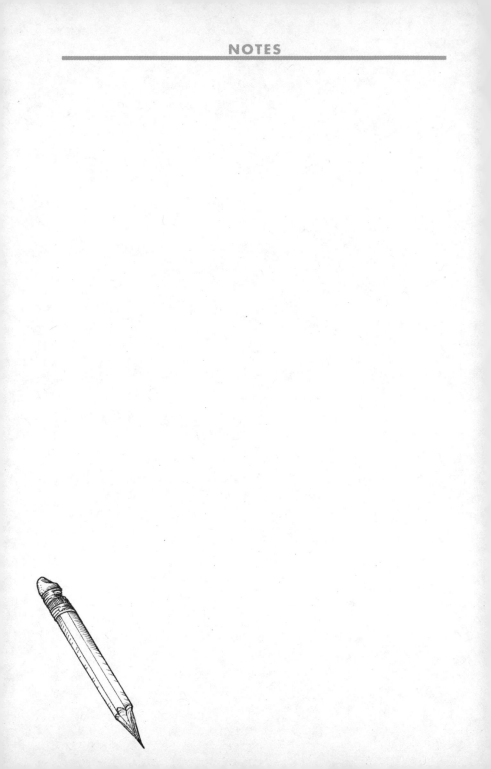

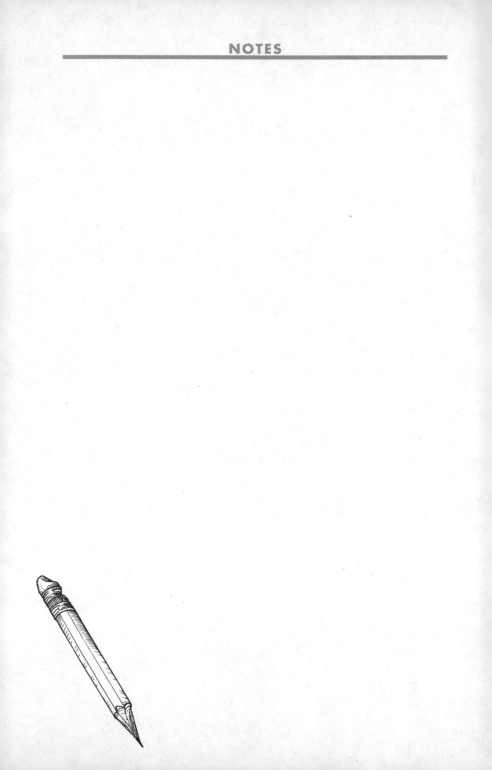